HAL LEONARD

GUITAR METHOD

Supplement to Any Guitar Method

FLAMENCO GUITAR

BY HUGH BURNS

To access audio visit:
www.halleonard.com/mylibrary

Enter Code
4972-9021-9995-4325

ISBN 978-0-634-08815-5

HAL•LEONARD®
CORPORATION

7777 W. BLUEMOUND RD. P.O. BOX 13819 MILWAUKEE, WI 53213

T0055398

In Australia Contact:
Hal Leonard Australia Pty. Ltd.
4 Lentara Court
Cheltenham, Victoria, 3192 Australia
Email: ausadmin@halleonard.com.au

Visit Hal Leonard Online at
www.halleonard.com

CONTENTS

TRACK 1
"Fiesta"

INTRODUCTION

This book is intended to be an introduction to flamenco guitar for players with a basic grasp of guitar technique. It contains exercises that develop a solid foundation in basic flamenco guitar techniques, such as *rasgueado*, *picado*, *ligado*, and *golpe*, among others. We'll also explore the different rhythmic forms of flamenco, such as *soleares*, *malagueña*, *farruca*, *tarantas*, and *rumba*.

Let's start this exploration of flamenco guitar with a question:

How do we find a way into the sound world of the flamenco guitar?

If you lived in Andalusia, Spain, you would be hearing the unique rhythms and sounds of Spanish and flamenco music, and your feeling for the music would develop in a natural way. If you're not this fortunate, however, it doesn't mean that you can't assimilate key forms and techniques in the same way. By seeing live performers, attending workshops, and listening, you will gradually absorb many aspects of the music.

Traditionally, flamenco is taught by listening and watching. The teacher plays slowly, and the student follows, gradually playing in unison. When the student has a good command of rhythm, he/she then begins to accompany dancers, which helps him/her understand the form of the various set pieces.

In recent times, written transcriptions of the major styles have become available. This has given reading musicians a way to experience this type of music. However, even a very skilled classical player will not sound truly authentic by simply playing the notes as they appear on the page, as the style contains a number of special techniques.

This book provides a way into this unique sound world by presenting some of the basic approaches, which will enable beginners to develop a strong foundation on which to build their knowledge of this wonderful art form.

A BRIEF HISTORY OF FLAMENCO

The roots of flamenco can be traced back to Indian, Arabic, North African, and even Roman influences. Nomadic travellers arriving in southern Spain brought these influences with them, and in combination with the indigenous culture (already heavily influenced by the Moorish occupation), a rich mix of art, literature, architecture, music, song, and dance developed. All of these factors and more have contributed to "el arte flamenco."

In areas like Cádiz, Ronda (Triana), Seville, Malaga, and Granada, a special way of singing and dancing evolved to express the experiences of the *gitanos* (Spanish gypsies) living in the poorer quarters of the cities. Flamenco developed at gatherings of family or friends, becoming a mechanism for sharing feelings through music and dance.

Around the 1840s, specialist cafés were opened in Seville that began to employ flamenco performers to sing and dance. It was in this environment that the role of the guitar started to grow. Though it was still principally used to accompany the singing and dancing, it also started to develop as a solo instrument. This café culture started to decline around the 1920s.

When the Spanish civil war began in 1936, a number of flamenco artists moved out of Spain, taking their music with them. Later, in the mid-1950s, many well-known artists made recordings, enabling a wider audience to hear the music. Festivals and competitions also developed around this time, allowing more people to hear the outstanding artists of the day and providing a platform of opportunity and training for the next generation of performers.

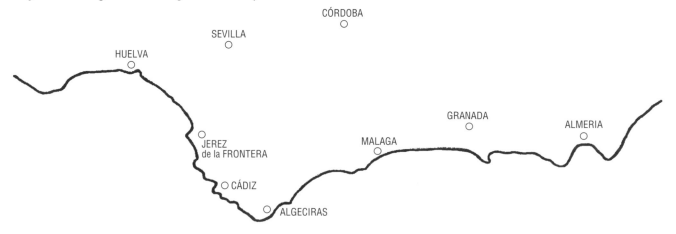

THE KEY ELEMENTS OF FLAMENCO

The flamenco style has three key elements:

1. *cante* (song),
2. *baile* (dance), and
3. *toque* (guitar).

A singer is known as a *cantador*, while *bailador* and *bailadora* are male and female dancers. The guitarist is called the *tocador* or *guitarrista*.

In addition to these elements, *palmas* (hand claps), *jaleos* (shouts), finger snapping, tap-ping on the table, and words of encouragement from the audience all contribute to creating the special atmosphere of a flamenco performance. At its best, performers and audience both participate, blurring the line between them.

A BRIEF HISTORY OF FLAMENCO GUITAR MAKERS

The design and shape of the modern classical guitar is often credited to Antonio de Torres Jurado. He also made a distinction between the flamenco and classical guitar. Manuel Ramírez (1866–1916) continued to develop Torres's ideas and taught some of the great makers, including Santos Hernández, Domingo Esteso, and Modesto Borreguero.

A new generation of guitar makers has now arisen, basing their work on the traditions developed by the early pioneers. Makers like Manuel Reyes, Contreras Gerundino, Fernández Montero, and the Conde Brothers all create guitars highly prized by leading flamenco players.

Don Antonio de Torres Jurado (1817-1892)

Don Antonio de Torres Jurado (commonly known as Antonio Torres—he adopted the "Don" as this was common for master instrument makers, and the "de" and "Jurado" were usually absent from his guitar labels) is seen by many as a pivotal figure in the development of the acoustic guitar in general. He is often quoted as being solely responsible for the form of the modern classical guitar and therefore many of the design features of modern steel-string acoustic guitars. He was possibly the first maker to clearly differentiate between the design of the classical guitar and the design of the flamenco guitar.

It's amazing to realize that Jurado pursued guitar making almost as a hobby. Starting at the quite advanced age of 33, he is thought to have only made around 320 guitars, of which only 66 are known to have survived. Because he wasn't able to make a decent living as a luthier, he first worked as a carpenter and then opened a ceramics and glassware store in Almeria, where he eventually settled.

Before Torres, guitars generally had a small, hourglass body outline, with the upper and lower bouts roughly the same size. To produce more volume, Torres introduced the much larger body with a larger lower bout. He used a system of fan bracing (still used in classical and flamenco designs today), combined with arcs in both directions, to stiffen the larger soundboard so that it could withstand the tension of the strings and emphasize the upper partials. He also settled on the longer scale length of 650mm. Unlike earlier guitars, his guitars were generally very plain and designed for the serious musician, forsaking the elaborate decoration found on "court" instruments in favor of tone, volume, and playability. (It has been suggested that the lack of ornamentation was due to Torres's limited financial resources, since he is known to have built some "exhibition" guitars with very detailed ornamental inlays.)

Although Torres was clearly a very talented luthier, many of the innovations he built into his guitars were also in use among his contemporaries. For example, although he is often credited as the originator of fan bracing, such bracing appears in Spanish-made instruments as far back as 1750. What does seem to be true is that he was a keen and methodical experimenter and gradually improved his instruments through testing and refining various techniques. He built a "Chinese puzzle" guitar that could be disassembled, placed into a shoe box, and re-assembled without the need of glue. He also experimented with a device he called the "Tornavoz." This was a steel cylinder fitted to the soundhole, extending into the guitar. It has been reported as an effort to improve projection, but in fact it would have acted as a classic Helmholtz resonator tuned port, altering the main bass resonance of the guitar. Another experimental guitar, built in 1862, had papier mâché back and sides to prove that, in a properly-constructed guitar, the back and sides had no significant impact on the sound.

Although Torres seems to have been, by nature, a secretive man and did not attempt to pass on his skills through an apprentice or associates, he himself did not feel he possessed any key secrets to building great instruments. In a letter he wrote to a friend, Juan Martinez Sirvent, he says:

"My secret is one you have witnessed many times and one that I can't leave to posterity, because it must with my body go to the grave, for it consists of the tactile senses in my finger pads, in my thumb and index finger, that tell the intelligent builder if the top is or is not well made, and how it should be treated to obtain the best tone from the instrument."

It is significant that a number of notable early Spanish classical composers and players used Torres instruments. Julian Arcas, a renowned composer and guitarist of the 1840s, helped Torres develop his guitars, and Torres guitars were played and treasured by Llobet and by Tarrega for their volume, projection, and tone.

KEY FLAMENCO GUITAR PLAYERS

- Francisco Sanchez of Cádiz (1840–1910), also known as "Paco El Barbero," is known to have played several *falsetas* creating extended solo passages and is said to be one of the first players to play solo flamenco guitar. In the early days of flamenco, the playing was based mostly on thumb and rasgueado technique.

- Paco de Lucena (1855–1930) introduced picado, three-fingered arpeggios, and the classical-type tremolo (*p–a–m–i*).

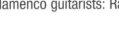

Paco de Lucena

- Javier Molina is a player of significant historical importance as his playing bridges the early and modern styles. He studied with Paco El Barbero in Seville and is said to have influenced two of the most famous flamenco guitarists: Ramón Montoya and Niño Ricardo.

- Ramón Montoya was born in Madrid in 1880. He served his apprenticeship in the cafés as accompanist to the most famous singers of the day and introduced technical innovations influenced by the classical playing of Tarrega and Llobet. His right-hand developments included complex arpeggios, highly developed picado, and a five-note tremolo played *p–i–a–m–i*. He extended the repertoire to include *rondeña*, which was a new form for solo guitar—all other guitar solos at the time were derived from song and dance forms (*cante*). A recording made in Paris in 1936 demonstrates many of these innovations (*Arte Clasico Flamenco* on the Hispavox label).

Ramón Montoya

- Although the trend towards technical virtuosity continued, a number of gifted players still followed the earlier styles, working with singers and dancers to create that special *aire*. Perico el del Lunar and Diego del Gastor were two who followed this path.

- Niño Ricardo (1909–1972) is regarded as a key figure for flamenco guitarists. As a youth he played with Javier Molina and throughout his career he worked with all the greatest singers, mastering every aspect of the art—both as soloist and accompanist. Almost all of the current professional players are influenced by the huge collection of falsetas he left in his recordings. Many guitarists have copied and developed his unique falsetas, thinking they were traditional.

Niño Ricardo

- Another maestro whose influence can be felt today is Sabicas (1912–1990). Although born in the north of Spain, far from Andalusia, his prodigious talent was clear for all to see from his debut at the age of eight. In 1937 he moved from Spain to America and lived in New York from the forties. The release of a record called Flamenco Puro in the fifties made him known to a larger audience. Sabicas has a special place in flamenco history as he set out to build a career as a soloist and put the flamenco guitar in the concert hall. Every aspect of his technique was impressive and continues to inspire each new generation of players.

Sabicas

BEFORE YOU GET STARTED

DO I NEED A FLAMENCO GUITAR?

Although a flamenco guitar will produce a more authentic sound, for the purposes of this book it is perfectly acceptable to use any nylon-strung guitar. The flamenco guitar looks very similar to the "classical" Spanish guitar; however, there are a number of differences. A flamenco guitar is much lighter in its construction than the classical guitar. The back and sides are thinner than those of the classical guitar and are usually made from lightweight cypress wood. This creates a brilliant (bright) tone, which is percussive, with less sustain than standard classical guitars.

The tops of flamenco guitars may be made of either spruce or cedar, with spruce being the most popular choice. The tops are also fitted with *golpeadores*, or tapping plates, to protect the surface from the nails of the right hand. You can buy self-adhesive, transparent, *golpeador* material, and it's probably worth fitting this to protect the top of your guitar from the impact of the tapping or golpe techniques.

On a flamenco guitar with a typical setup, the strings are closer to the fingerboard than usual. This creates a lower, faster action, or more immediate response, and contributes to the percussive quality.

Recent developments in flamenco guitar construction include the *flamenco negra*, which has a rosewood back and sides. These guitars have become popular with soloists as they have more power to project.

The traditional flamenco guitar used *clavijas*, or tapered wooden pegs, for tuning rather than the newer, geared metal tuners. Although most modern flamenco guitars now use metal machine heads, there are purists who insist on the old-style pegs. Besides the obvious differences in look and feel, the clavijas are also lighter than the metal tuning machines.

The two flamenco guitars used on the accompanying audio are typical of the current trend for modern makers. Both guitars are made by Conde. One has cypress wood back and sides, while the other has rosewood back and sides in the negra style.

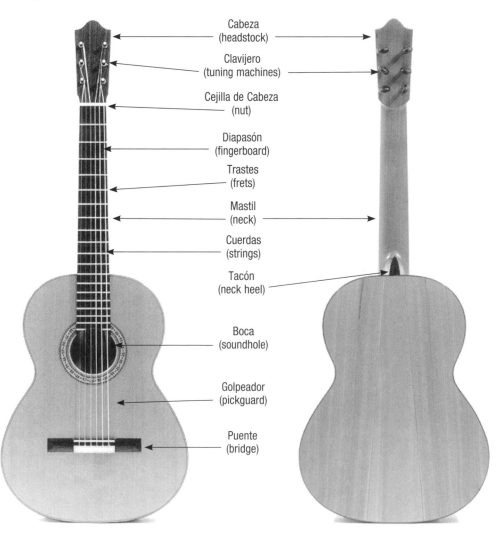

Cabeza (headstock)

Clavijero (tuning machines)

Cejilla de Cabeza (nut)

Diapasón (fingerboard)

Trastes (frets)

Mastil (neck)

Cuerdas (strings)

Tacón (neck heel)

Boca (soundhole)

Golpeador (pickguard)

Puente (bridge)

HOLDING THE GUITAR

Flamenco Posture

Classical Posture

Left-Hand Posture

Right-Hand Posture

Many flamenco players cross the right leg over the left and place the guitar's "waist" on the right leg. Paco de Lucia used this posture.

Paco de Lucia

FINGERNAILS

The fingernails on the right hand are a vital part of flamenco playing. The goal is to produce a clear, bright sound. In order to do this the length and shape of the fingernails have to be just right, although the perfect length and shape may vary from player to player. As a guide, the flesh of the fingertip should touch the string just before the nail.

Unlike other styles of playing, the back of the nail is also used in the flamenco style. For example, in the rasgueado it is the back of the nails striking the strings that produces the attack. Therefore, the nails need to be strong and may even require artificial support.

A number of methods can be used to protect the nails from wear and breakage. A nail lacquer (sometimes also called a nail hardener or strengthener) can be used to coat the nails. Many Spanish players use a type of glue which can be built up in layers.

Artificial acrylic nails, glued over the natural nail, are becoming very popular. However, using these artificial nails over an extended period can lead to thinning of the natural nail. Finally, rubbing a small amount of oil into the nails each day can help prevent them from drying out and from splitting. Miro Simic's nail care oil works well, as does olive oil, which many Spanish players use. Food supplements, such as gelatin and B-complex vitamins, can also help maintain strong and healthy nails.

TUNING

🔊 **Tuning Pitches**

TRACK 2

HOW TO PRACTICE

Here are a few hints to bear in mind when practicing. Try to follow this advice as you work through the book.

- Play slowly to warm up the hands.

- Use a metronome starting at, say, 50 b.p.m. and play a few scales.

- Use the right-hand thumb to strike the strings with a rest stroke.

- You should try to play in a relaxed fashion. If you feel tension building up, stop, rest for a few seconds, and stretch the fingers of both hands.

- Have a clear goal that you are trying to achieve. Look at the exercise and listen to the recorded example. Be sure of the left-hand fingering before you start to play the exercise. You will establish a secure technical foundation if you develop the habit of learning new pieces of information in this way.

- If you make a mistake, try to identify if the problem lies with the left hand, the right hand, or with your understanding of what you are trying to achieve.

- A recorder (cassette, mini disc, etc.) can be a great help to monitor your progress.

- Dancers often work in rooms with mirrors. This helps them to see the posture and movement clearly. The guitarist can benefit from using a mirror as well to check the hand positions.

- Playing along with recorded music, even if you only focus on the rhythmic aspect, can be a great help in getting the correct feeling for the music.

- Listening to recordings of great artists and attending concerts can provide much inspiration and is as vital to the learning process as playing and practicing. There are a number of wonderful recordings from both past and present masters.

The following list of albums will definitely inspire you:

Ramón Montoya	*Le Chante Du Monde*
Sabicas	*Flamenco Puro* (Hispavox 130076)
Niño Ricardo	*Maestro de la Guitarra* (Hispavox 4032571)
Paco de Lucia	Any CD
Tomatito	*Camarón Vivo*
Manolo San Lucar	*Tauromagia*
Vicente Amigo	*De mi Corazón al Aire*

SIGNS AND SYMBOLS

Arpeggio: Strum the notes of the chord in succession from low (bass) strings to high (treble) strings with the thumb, and/or with other fingers (as a *rasgueado*).

The ↑ symbol indicates a **downstroke**. (This is slightly counterintuitive, but is the convention adopted in all written flamenco music.) The thumb or fingers move from bass to treble strings in a single beat. If the arrow is in the opposite direction (↓) the stroke is from treble to bass (**upstroke**).

The sign ⌒ (known as a *slur*) can mean to play smoothly (*legato*), but more usually in flamenco it signifies a *ligado* (hammer-on or pull-off).

Capo Notation

The capo essentially creates a new nut—the fret above the capo becomes fret 1. So, for example, an E major chord played with a capo at the second fret is notated as a normal E chord, but the sound's pitch is actually F#. There's more information on capoes in the Appendix.

Left-Hand Fingering

1 = index or first finger

2 = middle or second finger

3 = ring finger or third finger

4 = pinky or fourth finger

Right-Hand Fingering

The following system is used throughout this book to identify the fingers of the right hand:

p = thumb (*pulgar*)

i = index or first finger (*indicio*)

m = middle or second finger (*medio*)

a = ring or third finger (*anular*)

c = pinky or fourth finger (*chiquito*)*

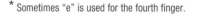

* Sometimes "e" is used for the fourth finger.

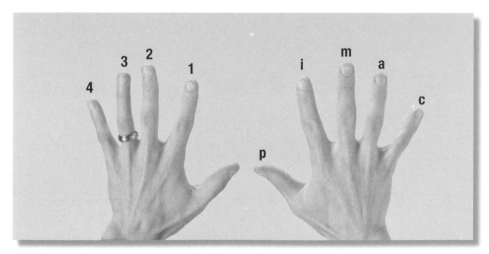

THE BASICS

Throughout this book, we'll look at the specific techniques and forms of flamenco, combining them in a series of authentic examples, which culminate in a final rumba at the end of the book.

THE E CHORD STRUM

Let's begin by playing E major. Use the right-hand thumb to strum the chord.

Now let's shift this same chord shape one fret higher. This chord is properly named Fmaj7#11, but for now we're just going to call it the "flamenco chord." Try it now:

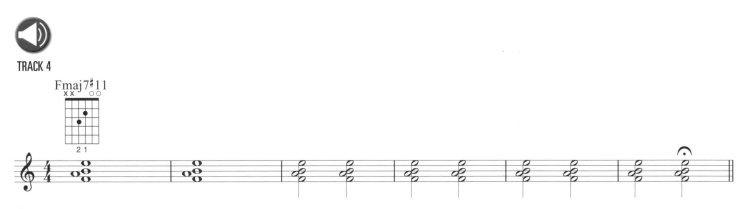

Now trying playing a sequence using these two chords. We've instantly created a typical Spanish sound using only this simple movement.

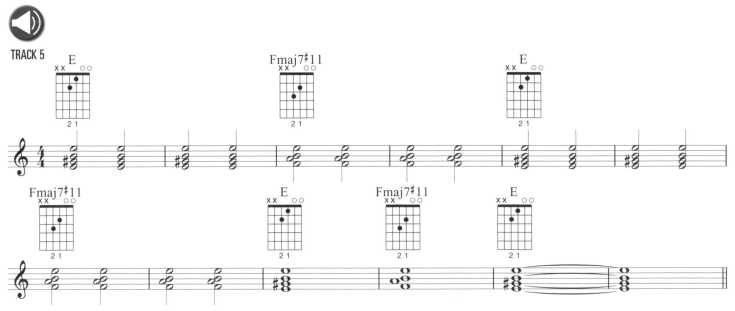

THE SPANISH CADENCE

The following chord sequence establishes a characteristic sound used in many pieces of flamenco music. The basic progression is Am–G–F–E.

This example introduces some barre chords (Am, G, and F). The term *barre* refers to the use of a left-hand finger (most often the first finger) to hold down a group of strings. In a full barre, all six strings are held down, although in standard tuning other fingers are used in front of the barre to form chords. It may take a little practice to develop the strength needed to hold down all the strings with the first finger. If you find it difficult at first, keep working on the simpler examples, and gradually the finger will become stronger.

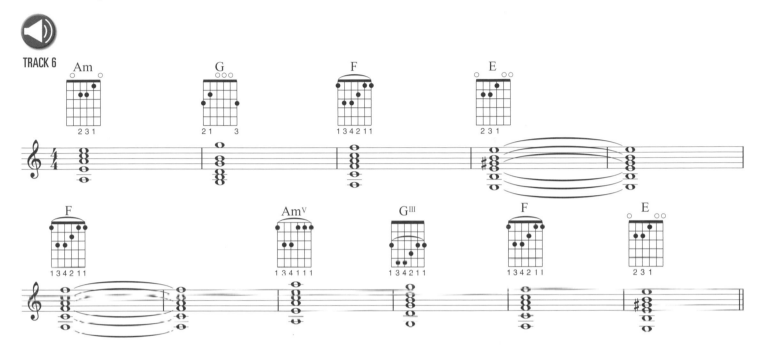

TRACK 6

CADENCE

In the context of this book the term *cadence* refers to a harmonic progression or a sequence of chords. The literal meaning, "a falling" (from the Latin, *cado*, I fall), was used to indicate a resting point or closure within a sequence of chords.

MUTED STRUMS

Now let's look at the rhythmic aspect of one of the most important forms: *soleares*. This is played by muting or dampening the strings with the left hand while strumming with the right. The rhythmic structure is based on a 12-beat cycle with accents on beats 3, 6, 8, 10, and 12:

1 2 **3** 4 5 **6** 7 **8** 9 **10** 11 **12**

TRACK 7
slow

TRACK 8
faster

See page 16 for more on the soleares form.

AYUDADO

AYUDADO (Thumb and Index Finger)

The thumb and index finger can be used to play *arpeggios* and single-note lines. (See more on arpeggios on page 17.)This technique was used a great deal by early flamenco players. It creates a very special sound and gives musical phrases a certain accent that is typical of flamenco. Ayudado also serves as a great foundation for other key techniques like *alzapúa* and for the use of *apoyando* (rest strokes) in the tremolo. We'll touch more on those later!

Try this simple exercise using the E and F shapes you've already learned. Let the notes ring throughout.

TRACK 9

In this exercise the thumb and index finger are used to play a melodic phrase. This can also be practiced using only the thumb.

TRACK 10

LIGADO

LIGADO (HAMMER-ONS AND PULL-OFFS)

With a *hammer-on*, a note (fretted or open string) is first plucked by the right hand in the usual way. Then another left-hand finger is used to "hammer" down onto a higher-pitched fret on the same string, causing that new note to sound. A *pull-off* is essentially the opposite of a hammer-on. A left-hand finger "pulls off" from a fretted note (down towards the floor), thereby plucking the string and causing a lower note (that's already fretted) or an open string to sound. These techniques are referred to in flamenco guitar as *ligado*.

Both hammer-ons and pull-offs are achieved with greater speed and force than the normal fretting motion. You'll really need to slam that finger down, for example, for a hammer-on to speak clearly. Here are some ligado exercises using all four left-hand fingers on all strings.

Repeat the exercise many times until it feels comfortable.

TRACK 11

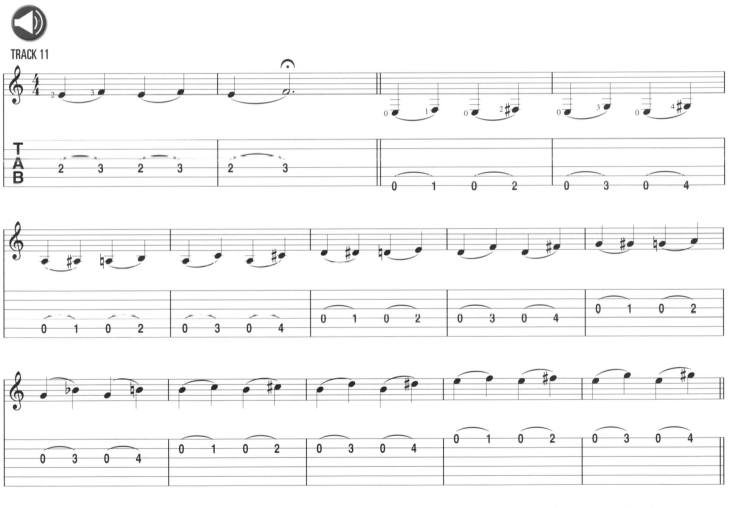

Here's a simple ascending pattern based on A minor using hammer-ons. It is played on the audio first slowly, then fast.

TRACK 12

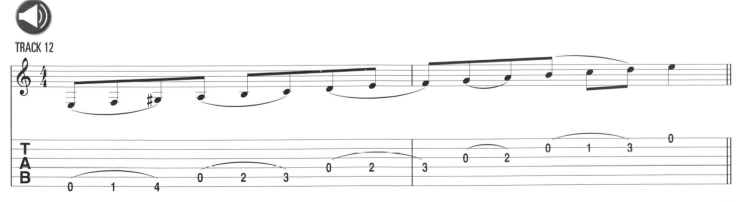

And here's a descending chromatic pattern to get you practicing pull-offs:

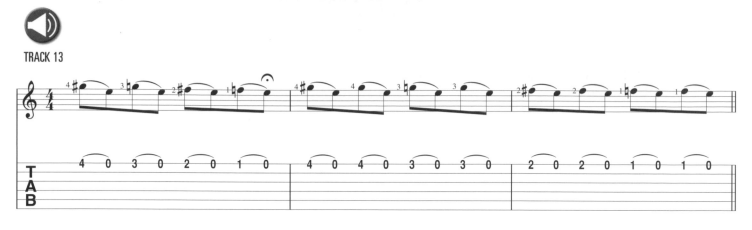

TRACK 13

[Music notation — descending chromatic pattern]

F----- here's a descending A minor scale pattern played with pull-offs. The example is played both slow and fast on the audio.

TRACK 14

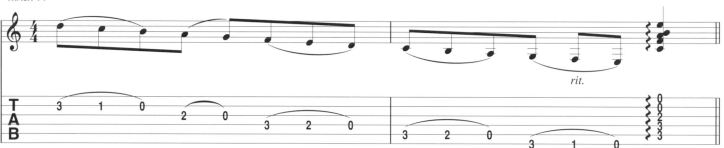

[Music notation — descending A minor scale with pull-offs]

SOLEARES

Now it's time to experience your first authentic flamenco form: soleares.

This soleares continues the technique of ligado.

TRACK 15

[Music notation — soleares]

16

ARPEGGIOS

An *arpeggio* is a sequence of individual notes from a chord. The following exercises cover common flamenco sequences. Repeat the arpeggios until they feel comfortable to play, then gradually increase the tempo. It is generally implied that you let the notes of an arpeggio ring together, as on the audio. Ramón Montoya is credited with being the first player to introduce the double arpeggio.

Descending:

Ascending:

Double Arpeggio:

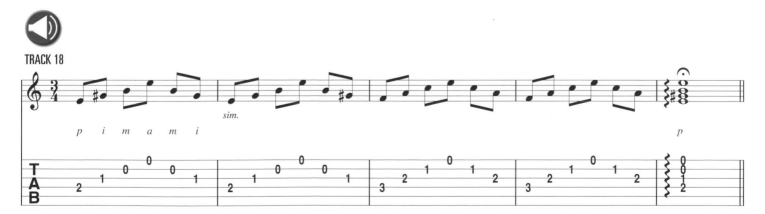

MALAGUEÑAS

The *malagueña* is another essential flamenco form and derives from the *fandango* from the city of Malaga.

The time signature of the malagueña is 3/4, but there are a number of different styles. For solo guitar (and even in vocal versions), the rhythm becomes more open (known as *en toque libre*—in free time), which gives the guitarist the freedom to improvise on the melodic or harmonic content of the piece.

In this exercise we build up the complexity gradually, starting with a simple bass line and adding a top-string pedal note on the upbeat before introducing a characteristic triplet rhythm. Two alternative right-hand fingerings are given for the third section; try both and see which feels most natural.

TRACK 19

18

RASGUEADO

Rasgueado (stroked or struck strings) is a word used to describe the distinctive right-hand rhythmic/strumming techniques of flamenco. It's vital to develop this technique, as it is such a characteristic sound of the style.

The word "strumming" doesn't really do justice to the many different types of rhythms that can be created. In fact, the literal translation of "striking the strings" is more accurate. You can play a single stroke with the index finger (or *m* or *a* fingers), a three- or four-stroke using all four fingers, or play from the wrist. We'll develop the technique incrementally over the following exercises.

INDEX RASGUEADO

Let's start with an index-finger strum. The strum moves through the strings from low to high (bass to treble) and down on the strings as if pushing them towards the soundboard. Try flicking the finger from a position just inside the thumb. We'll use the basic E and F shapes with which we started. The second half of the example uses upstrokes in between the downstrokes.

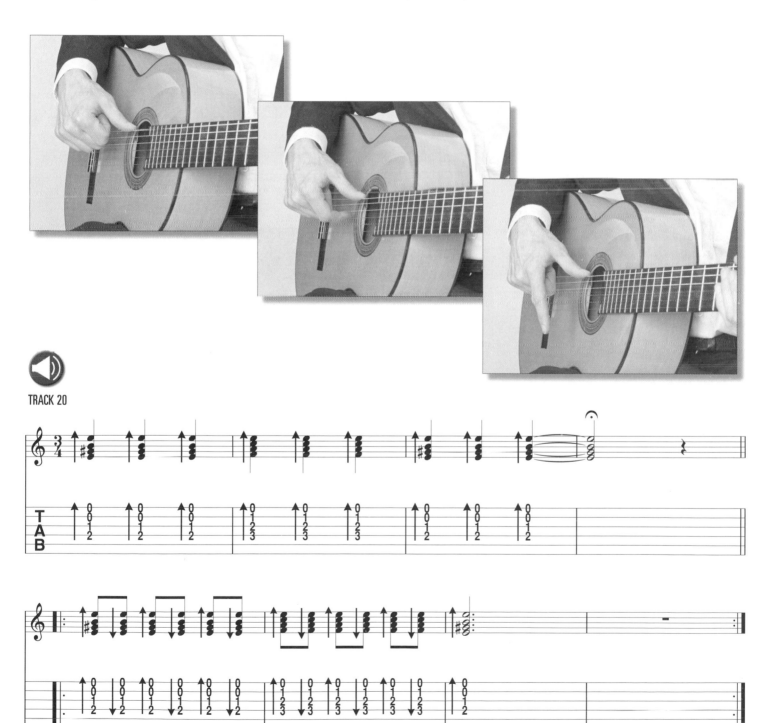

TRACK 20

MUTED RASGUEADO

Now let's try the same rhythm, but this time using the *i*, *m*, and *a* fingers and muting the strings. Lay your left hand lightly across the strings to deaden them. The movement in the right hand should come from the wrist.

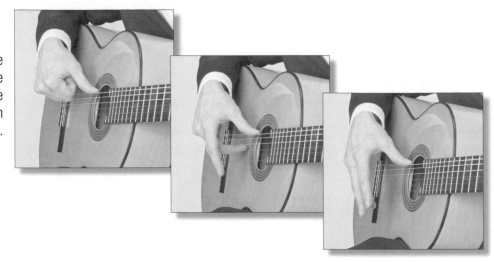

TRACK 21

FAN RASGUEADO

The *fan rasgueado* refers to using all four fingers and the thumb. This technique was used extensively in the past, but today the three-finger rasgueado is more popular due to its speed. However, practicing the fan helps to develop the whole hand, and it is well worth mastering.

The fingering is either *p–c–a–m–i* (with *p* as an upstroke) or *c–a–m–i–p*. Note the different symbol used here to indicate the rasgueado.

TRACK 22

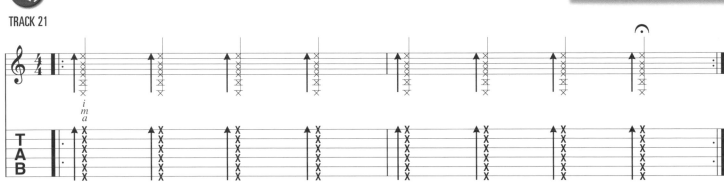

CONTINUOUS RASGUEADO

The *continuous rasgueado* is often used to begin a malagueña. It's a very powerful sound that really grabs the listener's attention. This style of rasgueado can be achieved in various ways. The *a–m–i–i* (repeated) pattern is often used, but repeated triplet or quintuplet groups are also possible.

COMPÁS

The word *compás* can mean a rhythmic unit or cycle, but it also refers to the form of a flamenco piece. Singers or dancers should learn the form and work within it; as the guitarist accompanies them, they too learn to play within the form. For example, in jazz, the 12-bar blues has 12 measures, and the chord sequence follows a definite pattern. Flamenco forms also have structures, which are vital to understand.

Within this book a number of the pieces are played in free time, allowing you to learn the playing techniques, which can then be applied within the structure of the dance form. When you are comfortable with the playing techniques it will be much easier to apply them to the structure and rhythm within the compás of the piece.

REMATE

The *remate* is an ending played to close a compás. Here are three possible endings that could be used with the malagueña you learned back on page 18.

TRACK 23

Let's return to the malagueña now and incorporate some of the new techniques we've introduced.

The first compás features apoyando, the thumb and index finger technique. There is a slow and fast version on Track 24. The fast version features a more liberal use of rasgueados.

TRACK 24

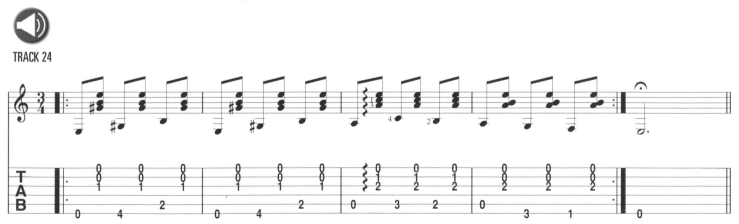

FALSETA

The *falseta* is a musical interlude, often played between the verses of a song or a break in the dance routine. A falseta can be melodic or rhythmic, and often contains a motif followed by a response that can then be developed, creating a pattern: question–response–development.

The second compás, or falseta A, is a bit trickier than the first compás, as it features higher positions.

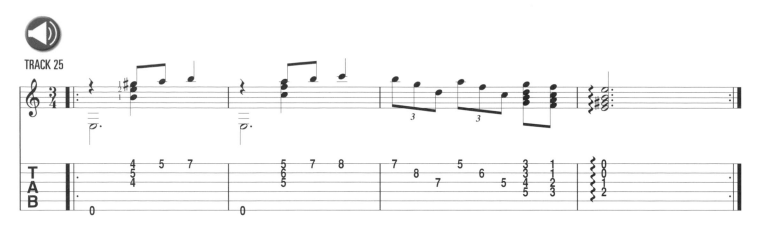

TRACK 25

And the third compás, or falseta B, features arpeggios.

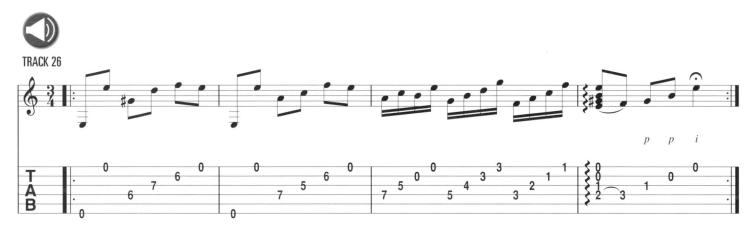

TRACK 26

Practice each of these three sections separately and slowly; once they are secure have a go at stringing them all together.

APOYANDO

PICADO

Picado means to pick the strings with alternate *i* and *m* fingers of the right hand. The fingers play the string and come to rest on the next adjacent string. This technique is known as a *rest stroke*, or *apoyando*, and is used for playing rapid single-note runs and slower melodic phrases. The thumb can rest on the sixth string to keep the hand stable while the *i* and *m* fingers play on the treble strings. When playing the lower strings the thumb should hold the same position but move onto the golpeador (protective plastic sheet covering the guitar top). The aim is to try to maintain the same overall hand position with the thumb providing support.

Here's an exercise to help develop this action. Start with the hand in position with the thumb resting on the sixth string and *i* resting on the B string. Try repeating each sequence until comfortable.

TRACK 27

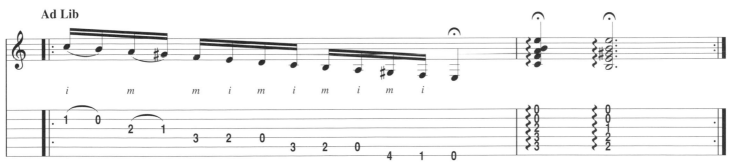

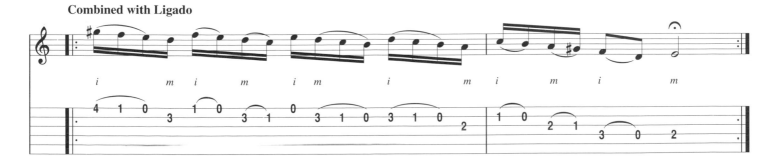

TWO SOLEÁS

Here are two more advanced soleá exercises. The first soleá breaks down into three compases. Track 28 demonstrates each compás slowly. Practice them all separately before building up the speed and joining them together, as demonstrated on Track 29. Notice the slight rhythmic variations in the faster version.

TRACK 28
SLOW

TRACK 29
FASTER

SOLEÁ

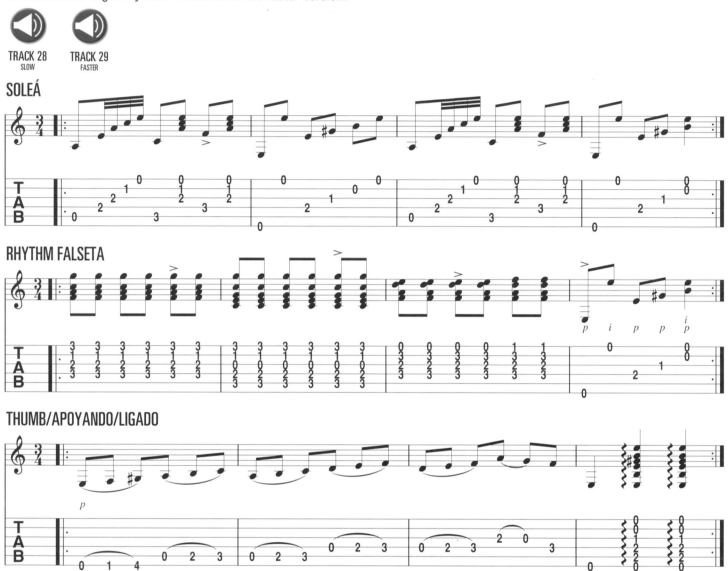

RHYTHM FALSETA

THUMB/APOYANDO/LIGADO

GOLPE

The second soleá showcases two new techniques. The first compás features the *golpe*: a tap performed on the top of the guitar. The golpe is indicated by a small square either above or below the staff. If the symbol appears above the staff the tap is performed with the anular (*a*) finger; if it appears below the staff it is played by the middle (*m*) finger tapping the top before hitting the sixth string.

LLAMADA

This is then followed by a *llamada*. The llamada indicates an ending or stop. In terms of musical punctuation, if remate is thought of as a comma, then llamada would be a period (or a half close as compared to a full close). The llamada can also be used as a lead-in for the singer or dancer, or at the start of the guitarist's melodic falseta.

SOLEÁ 2

LLAMADA

SOLEÁ 3

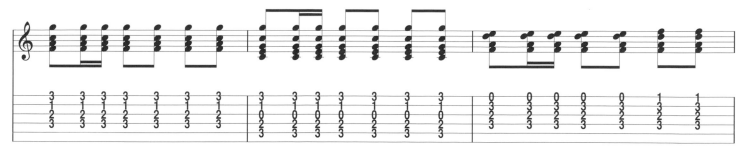

ALZAPÚA

This is a stroke unique to flamenco as it uses a down/up stroke of the thumb. The thumb plays a downstroke followed by an upstroke, using the back of the nail for the upstroke.

There are many different ways this stroke can be used: on single strings, on groups of notes, or using ligados. The following exercises will help you develop the correct movement. Remember to move the thumb quickly through the strings. The down-strokes of single notes are played as rest strokes (apoyando).

Note that the three following exercises use the capo—a device frequently employed by flamenco guitarists. See the section on "The Cejilla, Capodastra, or Capo" in the Appendix for more information. Where a capo is used, the written notes represent the open position. So on a guitar capoed at the second fret, an open fifth string is written as an A note, although the actual sounding note is a B.

TRACK 31

Capo II

*Capoed fret is "0" in tab.

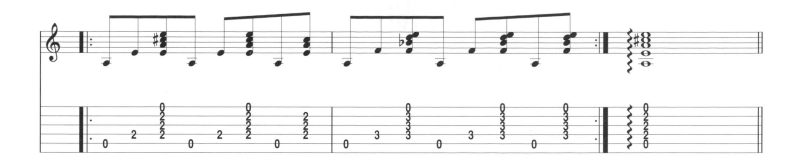

TRACK 32

Capo II

TRACK 33

Capo II

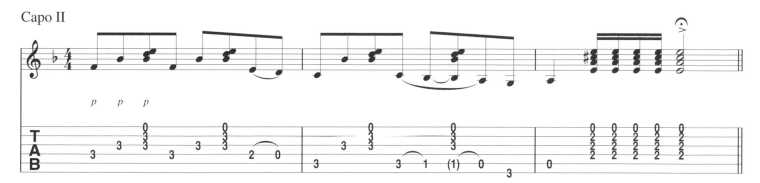

TREMOLO

The tremolo technique is used to create the illusion of a constantly sustained melody both in classical guitar music and in flamenco. However there are slightly different approaches to playing tremolo in either style. Generally, classical guitar music uses a free stroke with the thumb followed by three repeated notes on the treble strings, resulting in a four-note group. In flamenco the thumb uses a rest stroke on the bass strings and four notes are used on the treble strings, resulting in a five-note group.

The best way to practice tremolo is first to play slowly while aiming for an even sound. By learning to control the fingers at slow tempos, evenness and clear articulation of the notes can be achieved. Then when the playing speed is increased you will produce a smooth melodic line.

There is a clear connection between the hand movement used in tremolo and arpeggio playing. Working to improve arpeggio playing will help to control the fingers of the right hand. Finally, try practicing *p–i–a–m–i* on the first string. This one-string tremolo will help you observe the range of your finger movement. Practice slowly while aiming for small controlled movements. This is the key to developing a great tremolo technique.

Try the following exercises, which build from a three-note to a five-note tremolo. Notice there are several different right-hand fingerings that are usable.

TRACK 34

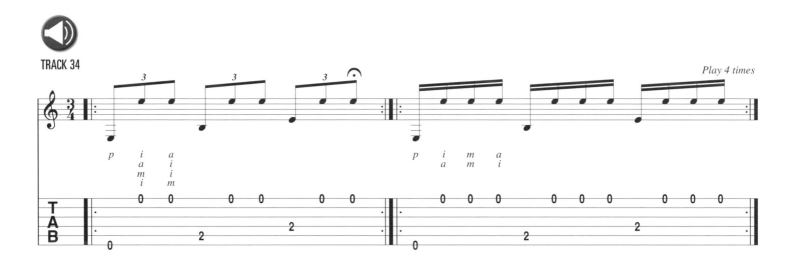

Here's a five-note tremolo demonstrated slowly and then at a medium speed.

TRACK 35

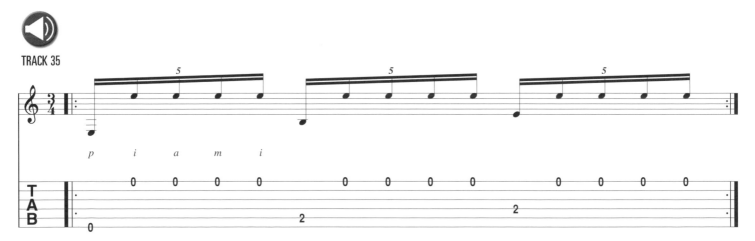

And finally, here's a fully-formed tremolo. Try this one as a four-note group as well.

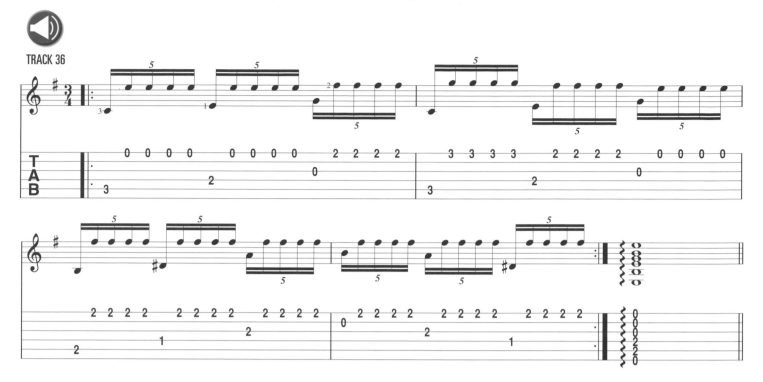

TRACK 36

APAGADO (MUTING)

Apagado means to stop the strings from ringing after a chord is played. This technique creates a staccato sound and gives chords a short duration with a sharp attack. There are two ways of applying the apagado technique.

One approach is to use either the little finger and/or another free finger of the left hand to dampen the strings after a chord has been played.

The second method is to use the palm of the right hand to stop the strings after the chord is played.

Use the following example to experiment with both methods:

TRACK 37

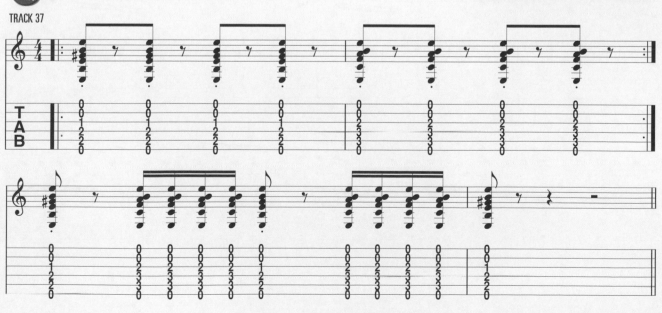

FARRUCA

It's thought that the dance form of *farruca* developed in Cádiz, brought there by travellers from the north of Spain. The rhythm is in 4/4 time, as opposed to the malagueña, which is in 3/4. In the traditional falseta, beats 1 and 3 are accented.

In the farruca the music can vary in tempo—some falsetas can have free melodic passages or driving rhythmic sections. The techniques used in the following example include octaves, tremolo, apoyando, apagado, and rasgueado. The tremolo can be played as a four-note to begin with. As this becomes comfortable you can convert this to a five-note group.

TRACK 38

RHYTHM FALSETA

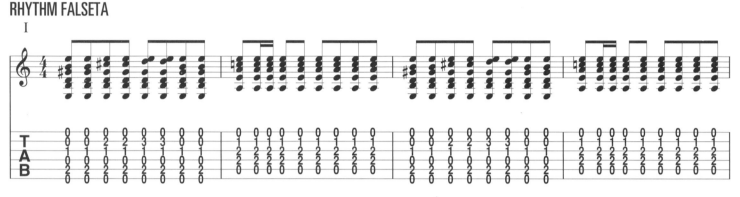

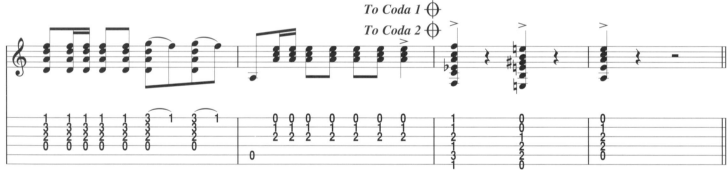

TREMOLO FALSETA

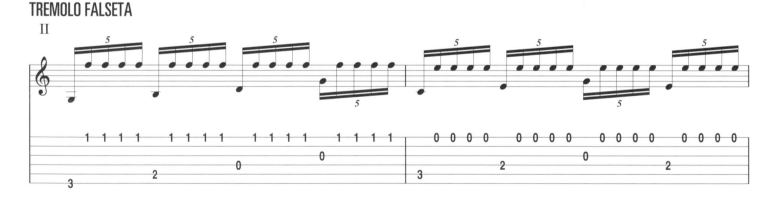

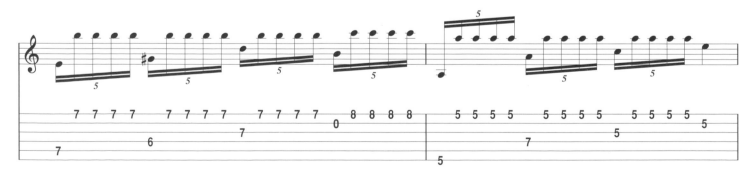

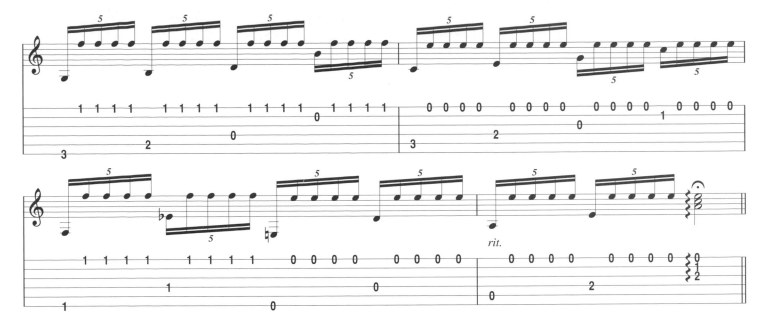

OCTAVE MELODY

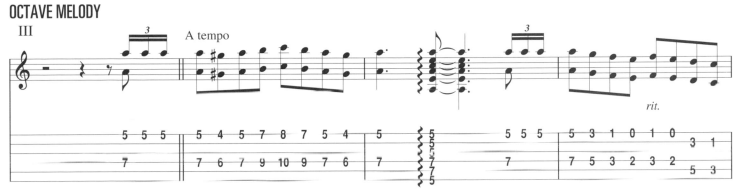

D.C. al Coda 1 ⊕ *Coda 1*

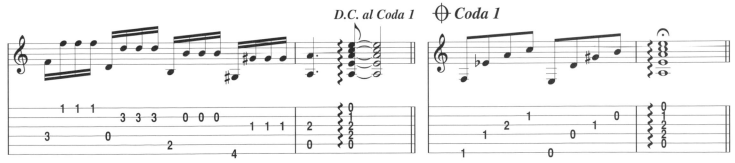

ARPEGGIO FALSETA

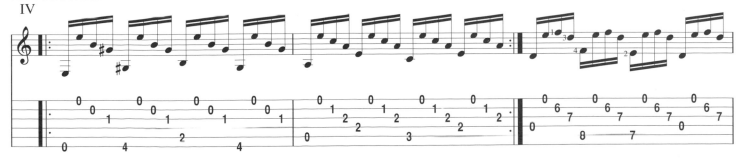

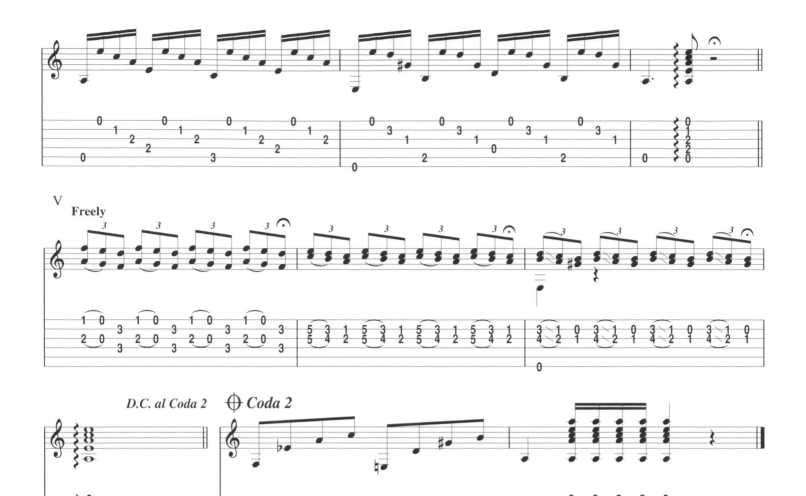

THE GOLPE REVISITED

As we saw back on page 24, the golpe is a percussive technique that involves tapping on the table of the guitar (or more correctly, on the golpeador, the protective plastic sheet covering the top), and can be used to accent the rhythm. It can also be performed while playing a downstroke with *i* or *p*.

Practice this stroke again to get the feel for it, as it can be difficult at first.

Track 39 demonstrates different ways of playing the golpe. (Each technique is demonstrated twice):

TRACK 39

1. with the fingertip

2. with nail and fingertip

3. with back of nail above soundhole

4. downward index finger with golpe on beat 2

5. combined with rasgueado

6. index finger strum with simultaneous golpe

7. with chords

    A. golpe on each beat

    B. golpe on beats 2 and 3

TARANTAS

The *tarantas* is a *toque libre* form. It has its roots in the regions of Almeria and Cartegena. The harmony used in this form is very distinctive due to the interval of a minor 2nd between the F# and the open G. This creates a wonderful tension and atmosphere.

TOQUE LIBRE AND TOQUE A COMPÁS

The term *toque libre* is used to indicate that a piece can be played in a free and open fashion. It may proceed with fixed rhythmic patterns for a while and then change as new chords or melodies are introduced, leading to changes in mood within the piece. The malagueña is an example.

In contrast, the term *toque a compás* means to play the toque (form) in strict time, as in dances such as the *buleriás* or the *seguiriyas*.

Here's an example of a tarantas featuring the golpe technique. Tarantas often features arpeggio, single note, and tremolo styles. Work on small sections to develop good control on the arpeggios. The 3/4 section is perfect for this kind of work.

TRACK 40

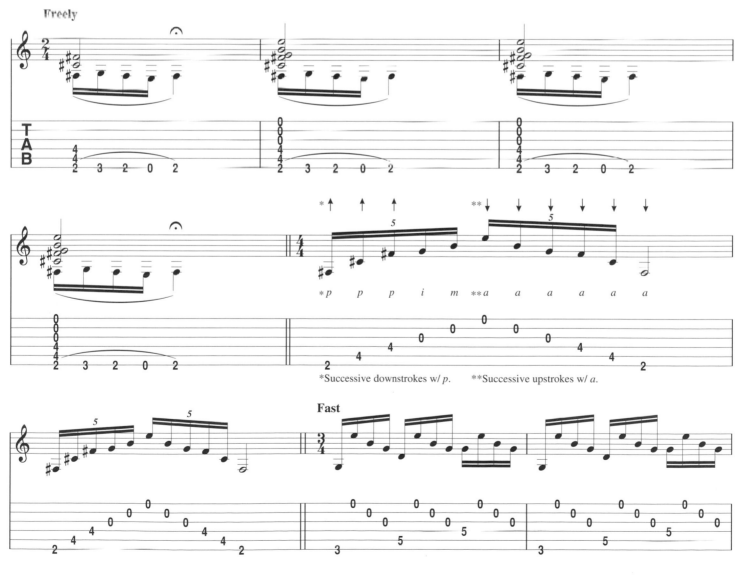

*Successive downstrokes w/ *p*. **Successive upstrokes w/ *a*.

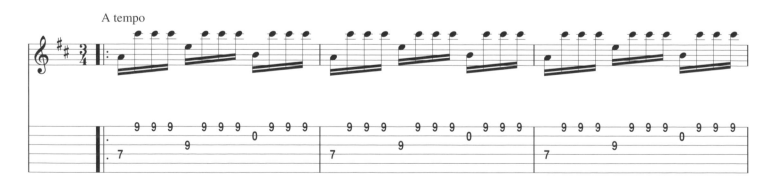

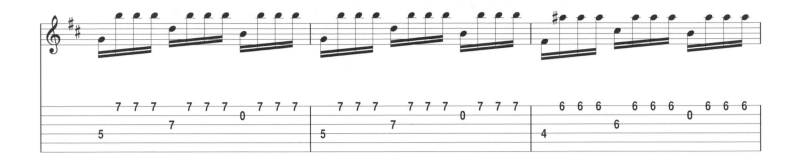

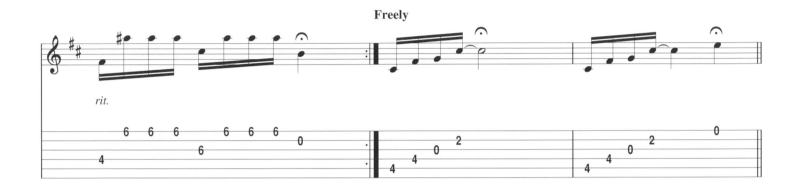

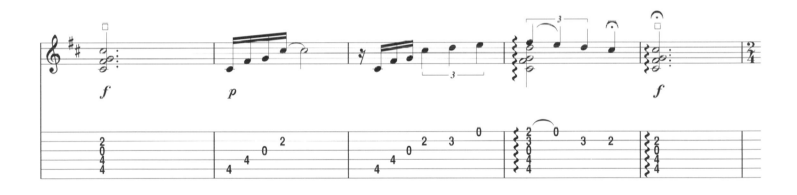

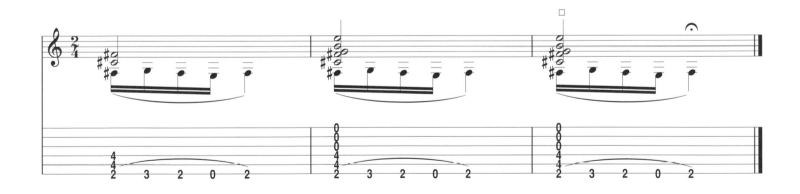

SPANISH CLASSICAL PIECES

Let's take a break from the technical side of things and have a look at some actual music.

THE INFLUENCE OF FLAMENCO ON SPANISH CLASSICAL MUSIC

It has been said that a number of the great Spanish composers—De Falla, Granados, and Albéniz, amongst others—were influenced by traditional folk melodies and flamenco songs. The melodic and harmonic content of their music is filled with wonderful examples of this. Manuel de Falla's *Noches en los jardines de España* and the *El Sombrero de tres picos* are recognized worldwide as quintessential examples of music with a strong Andalusian character.

There is a spring fair held in Seville where people gather on the streets singing and dancing many different types of *sevillanas*. The form usually has a rhythmic introduction followed by a short melodic phrase (*salida*). The full melody is then repeated three times. However, we are not looking at this form in detail here; we are simply drawing on the tradition written into the classical repertoire to develop a feeling for the "sound world" of this joyful music.

Albéniz's *Seville* is clearly based on a sevillanas folk dance and can give us an introduction to this dance form. Let's take a fragment of the main melodic motif and support it with some flamenco-style rhythms, as if accompanying a singer. Follow the chord symbols and slash notation above the staff to play the rhythm part.

There are some wonderful single-note lines in this piece that could be used as a basis for improvisation. The first melodic phrase represents a version of the original idea presented in E major, then in G major. The second phrase (sixteenth-note line) is a great exercise for the right hand using *i* and *m*. Also try playing this phrase using ligado to develop your hammer-on and pull-off technique in strict time. Note that the Tarrega classical guitar version of *Seville* is played in D–G–D–G–B–E tuning (fifth and sixth strings tuned down one whole step), but here it is arranged for standard tuning.

SEVILLANAS

TRACK 41

Albéniz

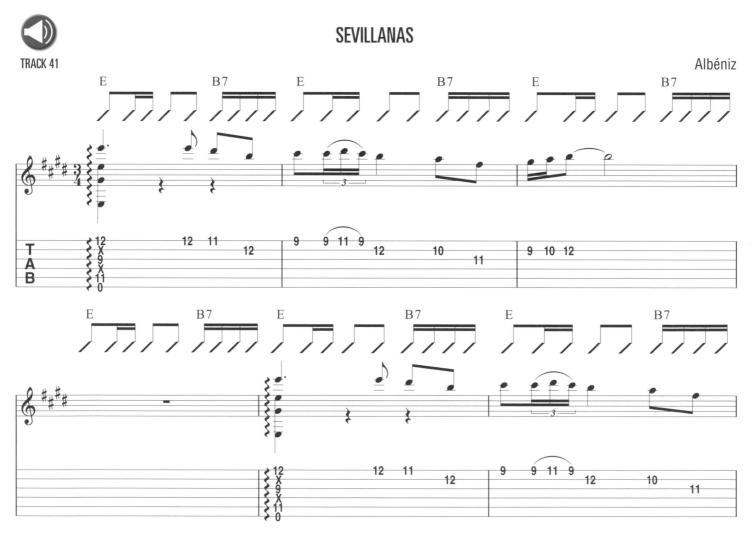

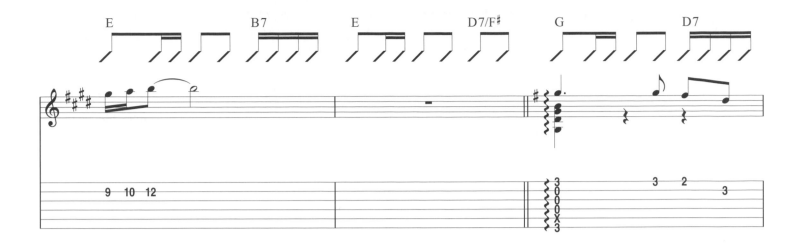

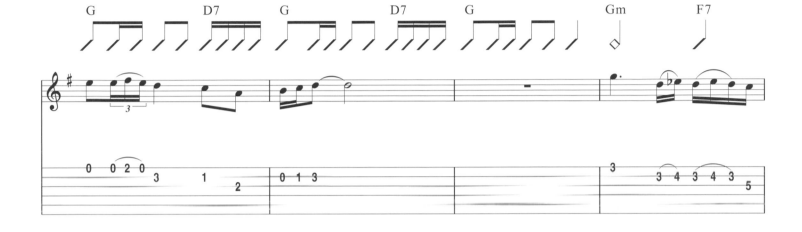

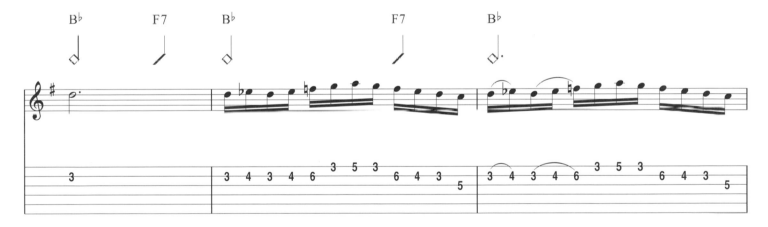

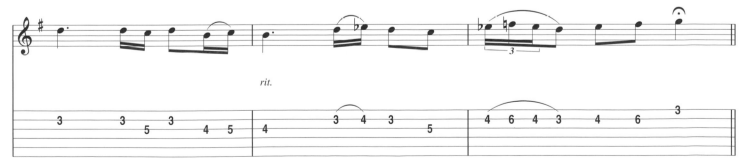

The second example is an excerpt from "Leyenda," also by Isaac Albéniz. This is a very famous and popular piece that has been played by many guitarists. It is typically Spanish in sound and seems to be perfectly suited for the guitar, although it is part of the *Suite Espagnole*, originally written for the piano. Albéniz was regarded as a great virtuoso pianist. He drew great inspiration from his travels around Spain, and many of his compositions have been transcribed for guitar. It is possible that some of his inspiration came from hearing fragments of guitar melodies and rhythms played by travelling street musicians.

The short excerpt given here, with its vibrant rhythm and strummed chord accents, gives the impression of spontaneous performance that is so vital in flamenco styles.

LEYENDA

TRACK 42

Albéniz

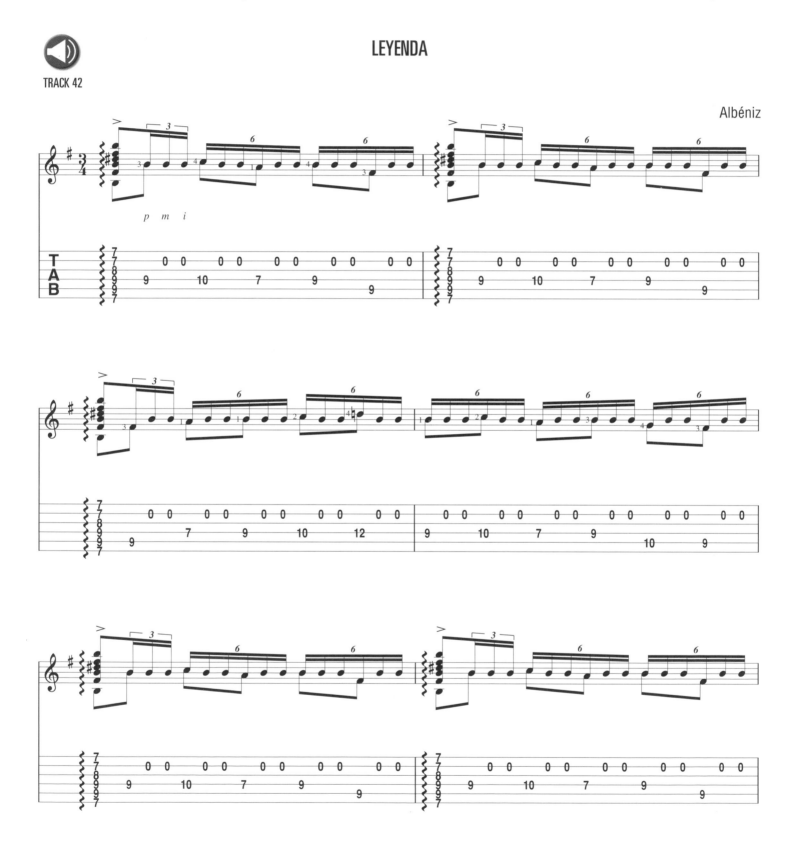

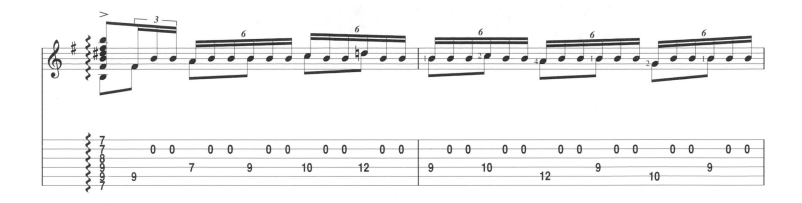

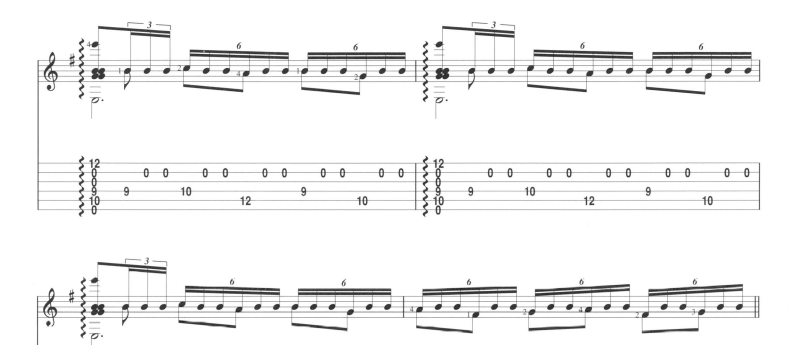

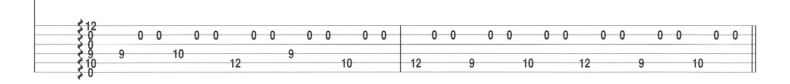

Joaquin Rodrigo, Manuel de Falla, and Enrique Granados are three other composers who have written wonderful music in the Spanish idiom well worth hearing.

RASGUEADO VARIATIONS

Here is a further variation on the rasgueado technique. There are many ways of playing this technique. Below are a few examples that give alternative ways of using the right-hand fingers. Try playing the examples with muted strings or an E chord.

Exercises 1 and 2 use finger rasgueados, while exercises 3 and 4 use a finger *and* wrist movement.

1

c   a   m   i   c   a   m   i

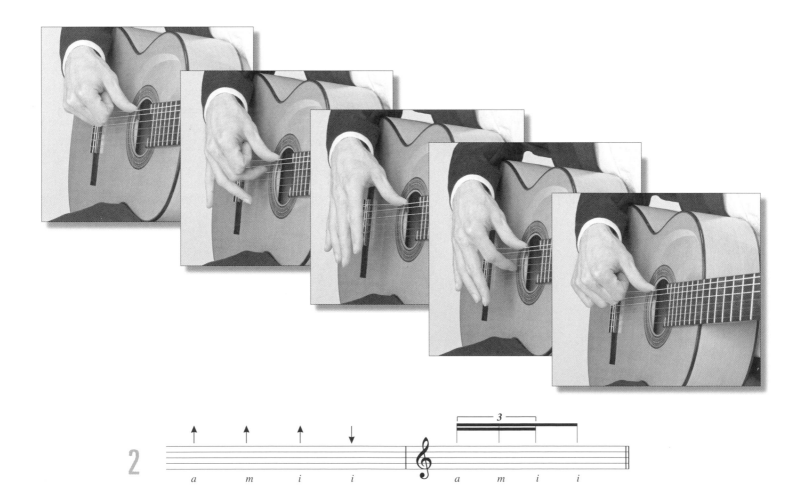

2

a   m   i   i   a   m   i   i

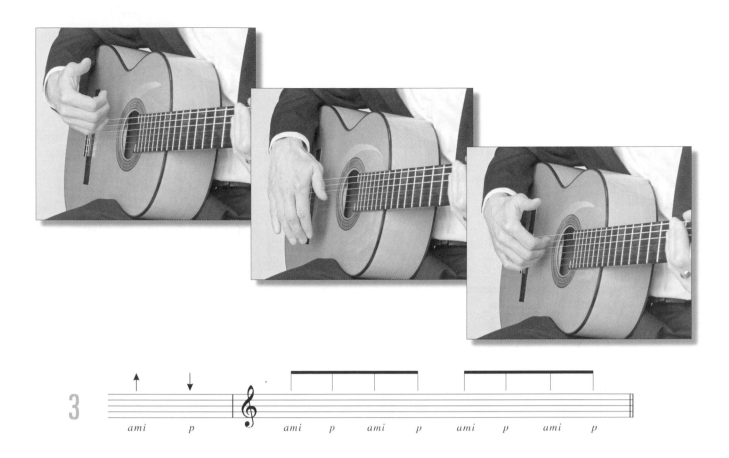

3

ami   p   ami   p   ami   p   ami   p   ami   p

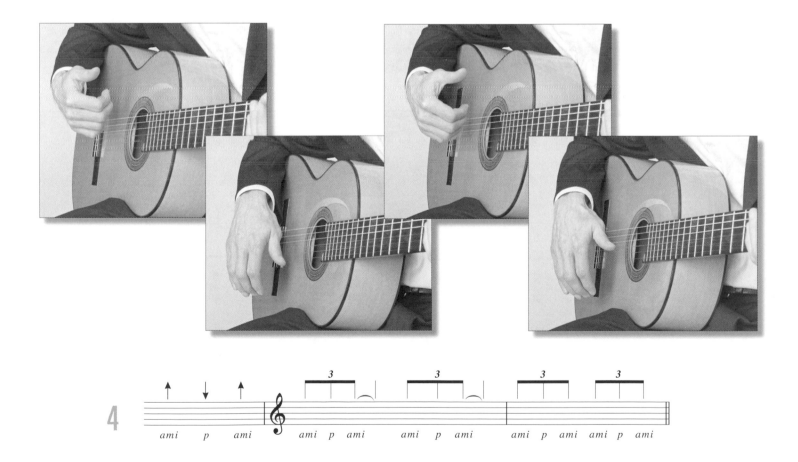

4

ami   p   ami   ami   p   ami   ami   p   ami   ami   p   ami   ami   p   ami

Here are two examples that will allow you to experiment with these different rasgueado techniques.

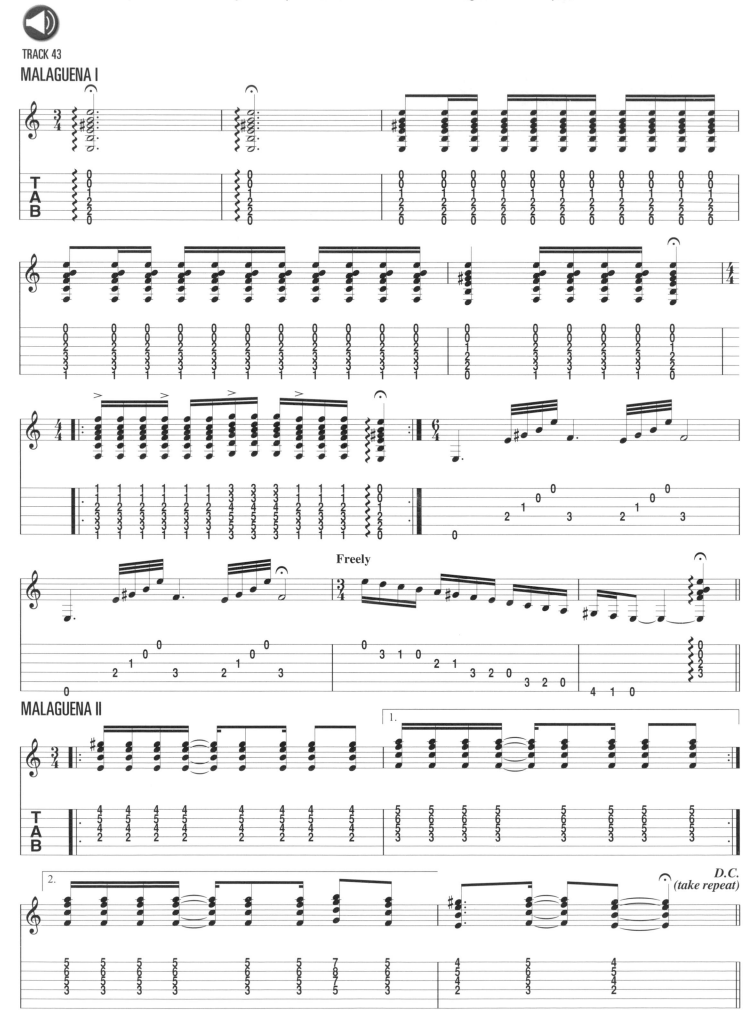

IMPROVISATION

Improvisation is a very strong element within the flamenco tradition. The guitarist is allowed much freedom within the structure of the form. If he or she is performing with a dancer or singer, different falsetas can be introduced between the singing and dancing. However, the rhythm scheme, or compás, must remain constant. The mood of the moment may inspire the singer or dancer with new ideas, and the guitarist can respond to this in his/her rhythm playing and melody/answer phrases.

In short, the performers should inspire each other through careful listening and observation. It is clear that a thorough knowledge of all basic dance rhythms is vital to act as a framework on which the improvisation can be built, just as a jazz guitarist playing over a set of standard chord changes may change melodic or harmonic elements while the basic structure remains constant. There are a number of modern innovations in flamenco where the solo guitarist introduces harmony from other styles of music and the rhythm may be more freely interpreted.

Learning as many variations as possible of the various forms is one of the best ways to gain a repertoire of ideas. Also by listening to the great masters from the past you can understand how they created their own unique sounds.

A practical approach to understanding improvisation is to break it down into the following:

1. Melody – the use of melodic phrases or motifs.

2. Rhythm – an understanding of different rhythmic groupings.

3. Harmony – looking at the chords and scales that help to create the unique qualities of the Spanish sound.

In the following example tracks, the first ideas we use come from the Phrygian mode. This set of notes is used in many flamenco forms. If our chord progression is in E minor, we can start the scale from the 5th note (B) to use a Phrygian sound. For example, B Phrygian contains the notes B–C–D–E–F♯–G–A. This scale creates melodies that give our playing a flamenco or Spanish sound when played with the backing track.

B Phrygian Mode

Any of the notes from the Phrygian scale can be played over any of the chords derived from the scale.

MODES

If we harmonize the B Phrygian mode we create the triads of Em, F♯°, G, Am, Bm, C, and D. One variation on this scale is to raise the third note from D to D♯, creating a dominant chord of B7. This one different note is responsible for giving the chord sequence the typical Spanish sound.

Harmonized B Phrygian Mode

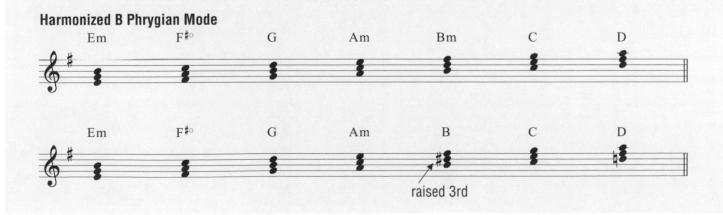

Here are three examples to help you practice improvisation:

Track 44 is a full demonstration with rhythm guitar and percussion.

Track 45 features percussion only so that you can practice your rhythm playing.

Track 46 is a double-length backing track for you to practice playing improvised single-note lines.

TRACK 44
full version

TRACK 45
percussion only

TRACK 46
double length

PHRYGIAN IMPROVISATION

TARANTAS REVISITED

Here is a further example of the tarantas, featuring a variety of more advanced techniques.

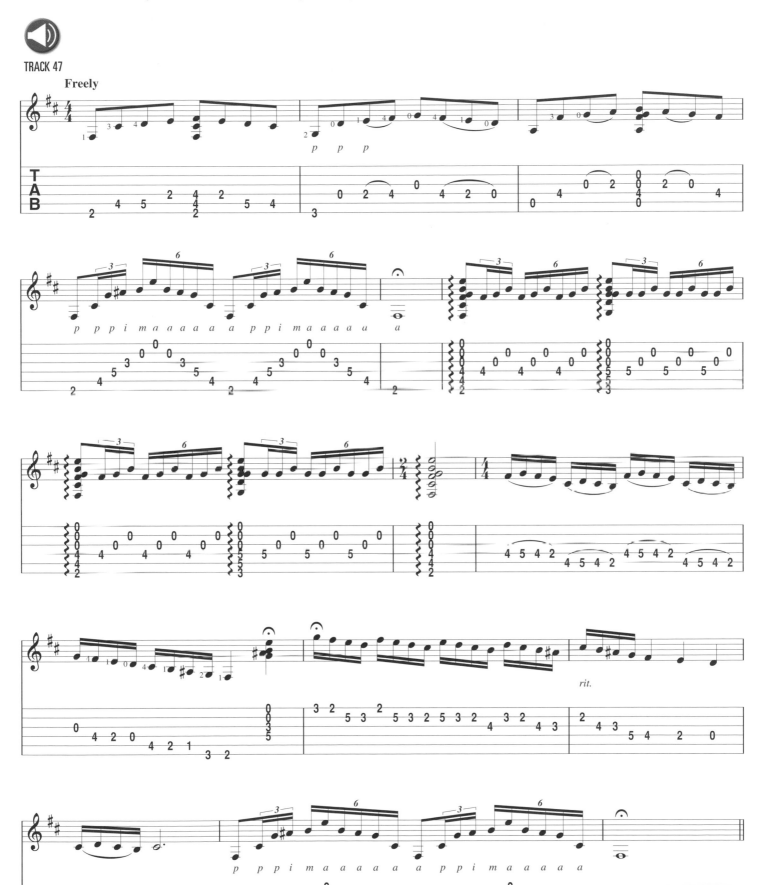

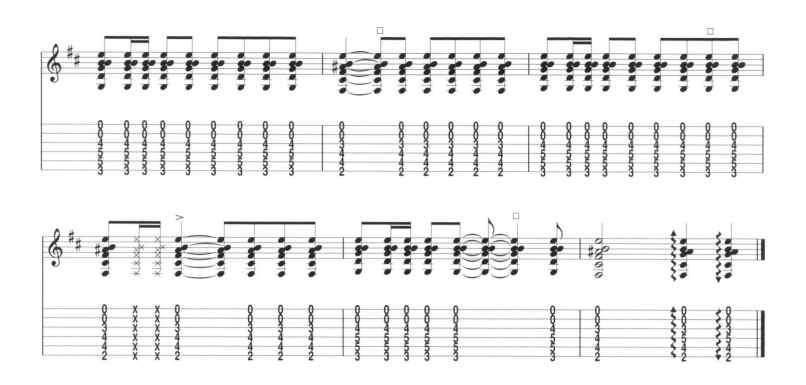

THE CAJÓN

The main percussion instrument featured on the backing tracks is known as the *cajón*. This instrument originally came from Peru and became popular in Cuba where there has been a tradition of playing packing crates as percussive instruments on the docks. In shape it resembles a large box, which the player sits on, striking the front of the box with his or her hands.

The cajón has become very popular with flamenco groups, as the sound complements the guitar very well. It's still developing as an instrument; some new models have a drum snare (or guitar strings) fitted to the inside of the playing surface to create a drum-like sound, while others have small cymbals or bells to add a high percussive edge to the rhythm.

TANGO

The *tango* is a 4/4 rhythm, thought to have originated from Cádiz and Seville. There are a number of variations and other dance forms derived from the basic tango form, including the tientos and the tanguillos.

The chord progression is Dm–C–B♭–F–A and follows a similar sequence to the typical Spanish cadence, however the chord types can vary. For example 7ths or 9ths may be added to the C chord, and 7ths and other color tones may be added to the B♭ and A chords. The C section is an improvised section based on the ideas used in A and B.

Again, this piece is presented in different versions on the audio:

Track 48 – Full version

Track 49 – Without melody (see page 50 for rhythm guitar part)

Track 50 – Without rhythm guitar

Track 51 – Double-length backing track (see page 50 for rhythm guitar part)

(Remember to use a capo at the second fret if you'd like to play along with the audio!)

TRACK 48
full version

TRACK 49
w/ out melody

TRACK 50
w/ out rhythm

TRACK 51
double length

Capo II

Intro

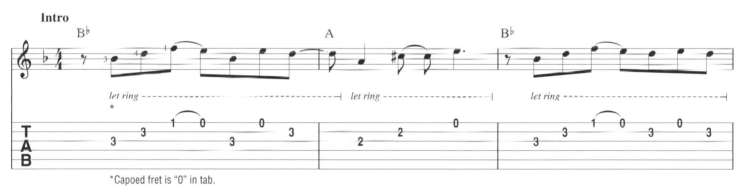

*Capoed fret is "0" in tab.

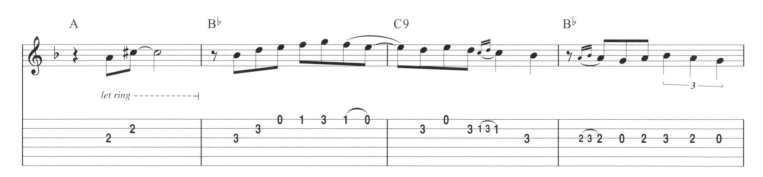

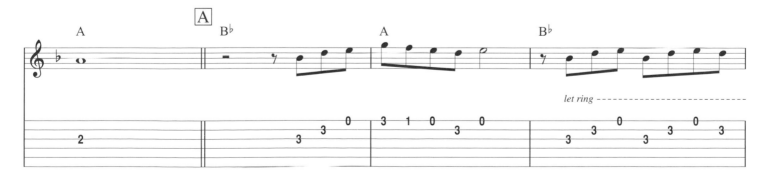

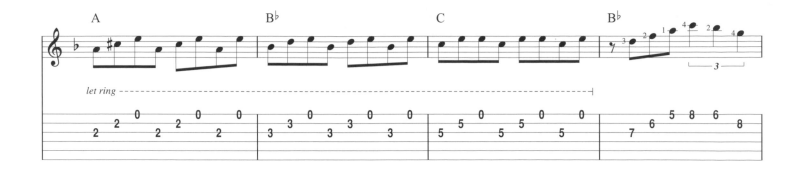

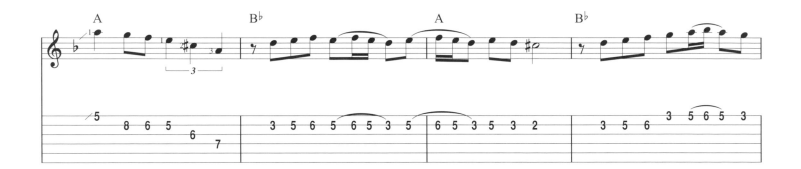

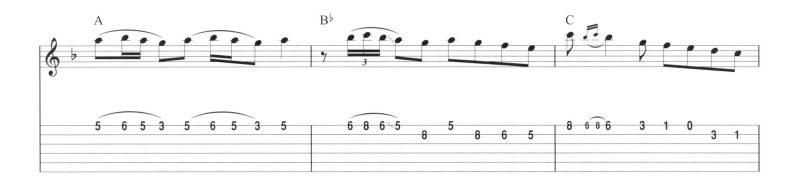

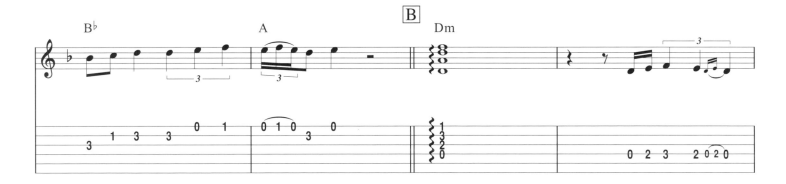

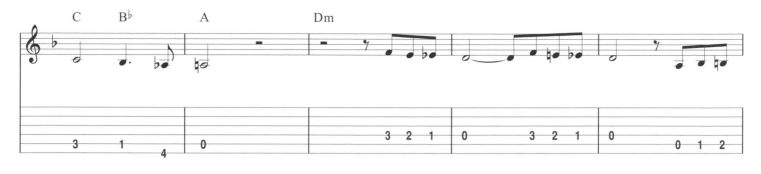

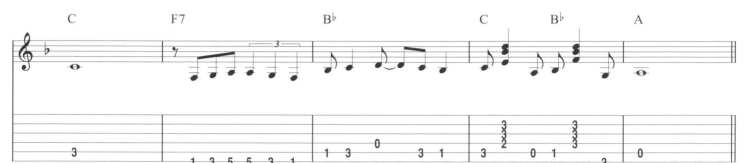

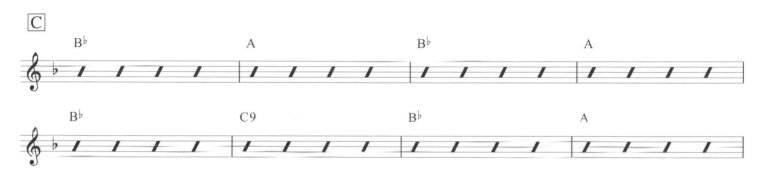

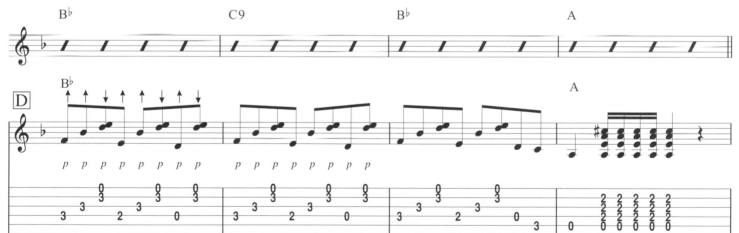

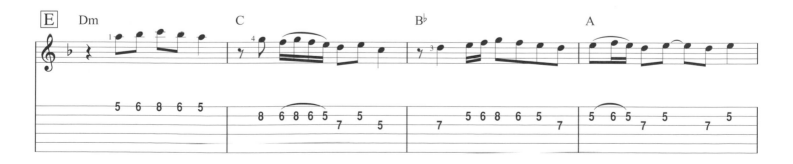

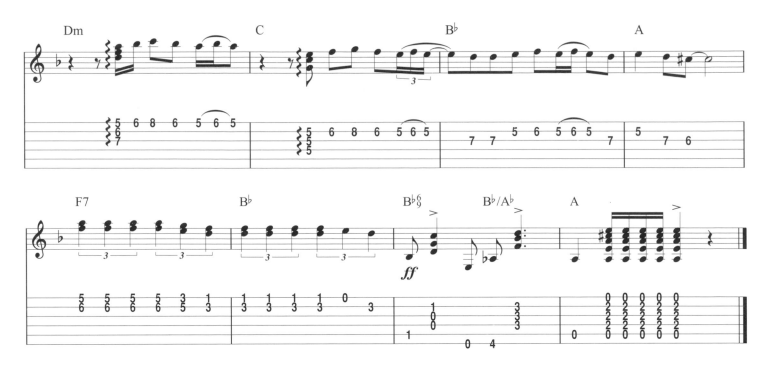

Here's the chord chart, if you'd like to play the rhythm part along with Track 50.

TRACK 48
full version

TRACK 49
w/ out melody

TRACK 50
w/ out rhythm

TRACK 51
double length

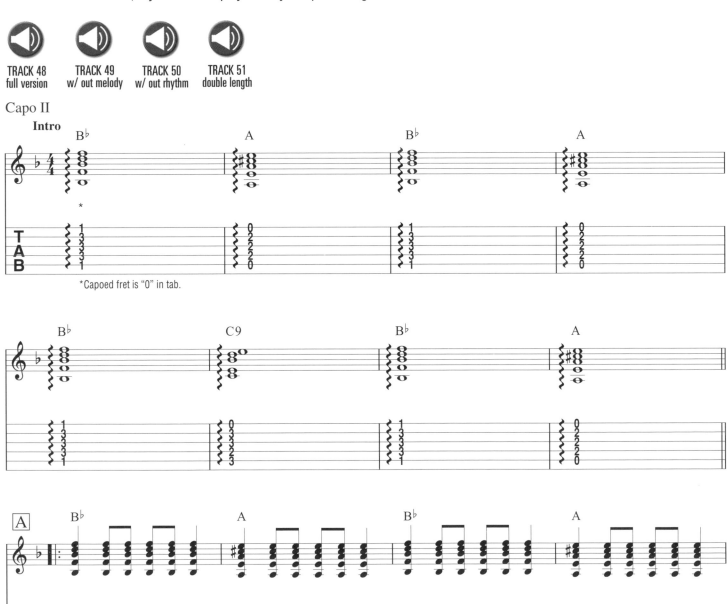

*Capoed fret is "0" in tab.

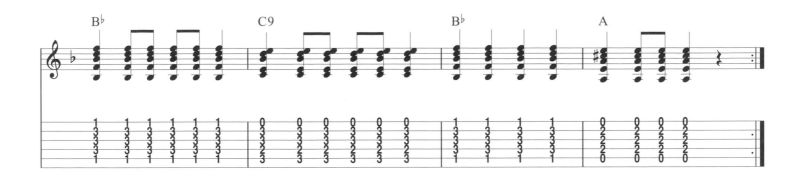

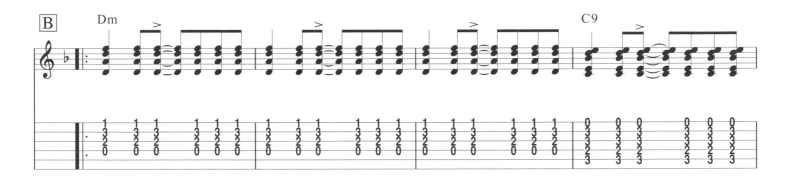

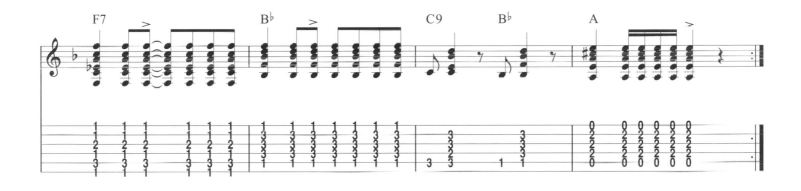

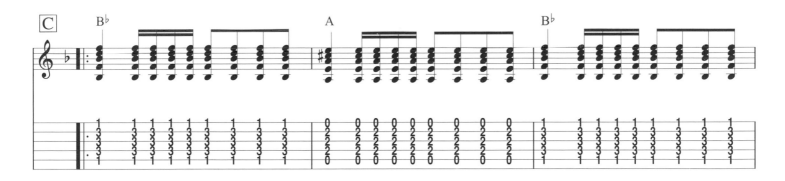

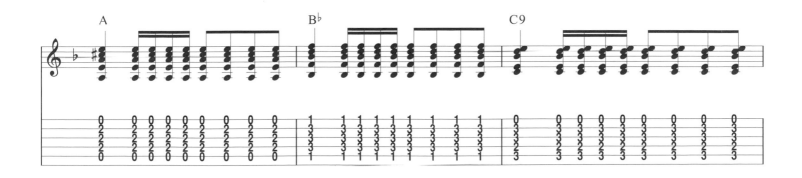

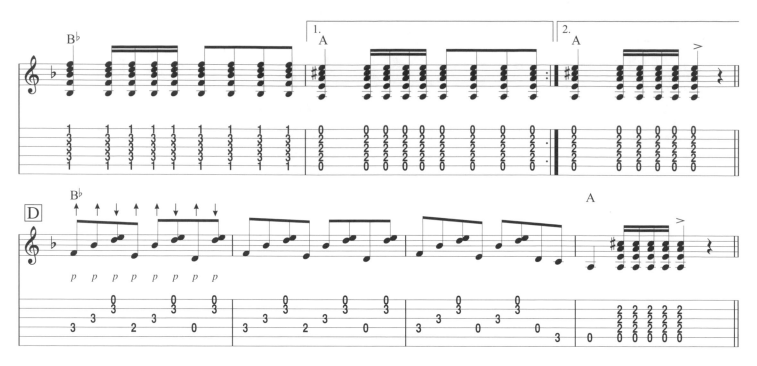

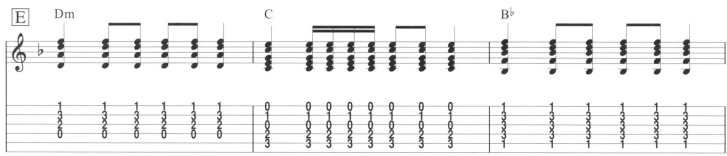

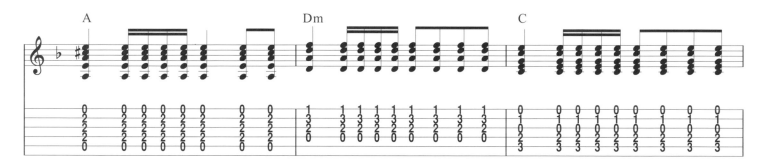

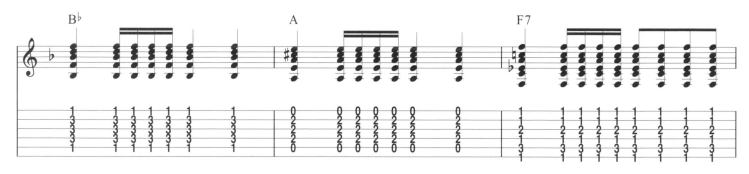

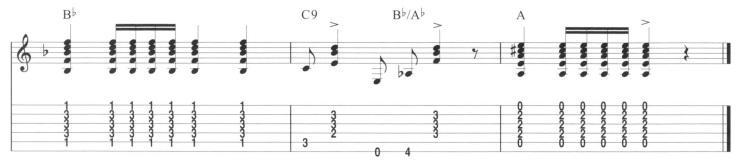

RUMBA

The *rumba* originated in Spain, travelled to South America, and returned to Spain with all the influences picked up along the way. Cuban music in particular is thought to have played a major role in the development of the rumba. Several other forms, including the *milongas* and *guajiras*, are known to have contributed to the modern form of the rumba.

A number of popular Spanish music styles use the rumba as the basis for composition. One of Paco de Lucia's most popular pieces, "Entre Dos Aguas," is built upon the rumba form.

There are three main variations on the rumba in flamenco:

- Rumba Flamenca
- Rumba Aflamencada
- Rumba Concertamenta

The rumba example presented here will enable you to work on rhythm playing with percussion and on improvising from a given theme. Listen to Track 52 to hear the overall feel of the rumba. Start by trying the rhythm part; begin with the first pattern and then try the different rhythmic variations.

- A: basic rhythm
- B: basic rhythm plus rasgueado
- C: arpeggiated version
- D: rhythmic version with golpe (played at two different speeds)

The last rhythmic variation demonstrates another type of percussive golpe stroke. The first beat in each group is played by tapping the soundboard lightly with the tips of the right-hand fingers (*i, m, a*). The hand is open, similar to the position for the apagado technique. The palm slaps the strings and the fingers hit the golpe plate at the same time. This is followed by an upstroke with the *i* finger; the *a* and *m* fingers continue the next down and upstrokes. This pattern is then repeated over the chord sequence.

Tip: If the right-hand slap is closer to the bridge it produces a lower sound; if you play it closer to the fretboard you can create a higher sound.

TRACK 52

RHYTHM PHRASES FOR THE RUMBA

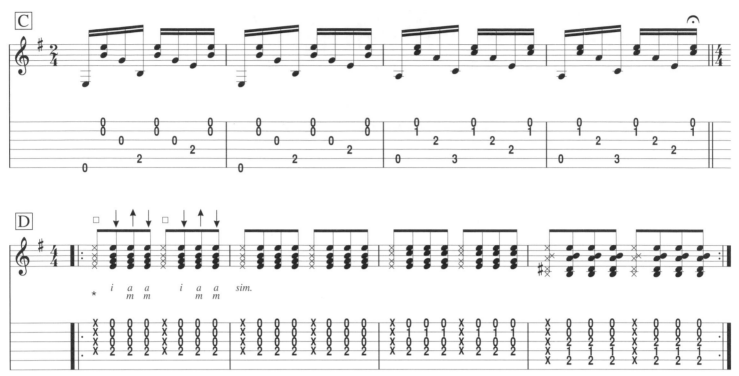

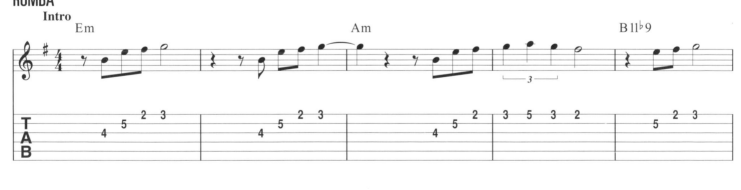

*Slap string w/ palm while tapping golpe plate w/ fingers.

Track 53 features a complete demonstration of the rumba. Try playing the melody first. The eight-measure introduction sets up the basic theme, which is then developed throughout the piece. The chorus features a melodic arpeggio section that shows how you can create melodies from within the chord sequence. It will take a bit of work to bring out the top melodic line.

The solo section gives an example of how you might develop a solo from a given theme. It's based on the verse and bridge chord sequence. You could try slight melodic and rhythmic variations to the written verse and bridge as a way to ease yourself into improvising.

The rhythm parts are all based on patterns demonstrated in Track 52. Tracks 53–56 feature alternate mixes that will allow you to practice the different parts.

TRACK 53   TRACK 54   TRACK 55   TRACK 56
full version   w/ out melody   w/ out rhythm   percussion only

RUMBA

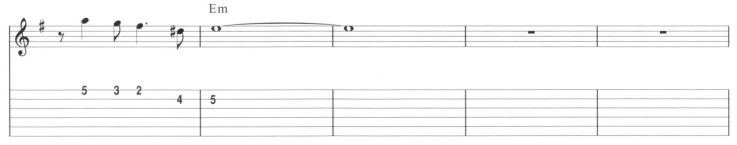

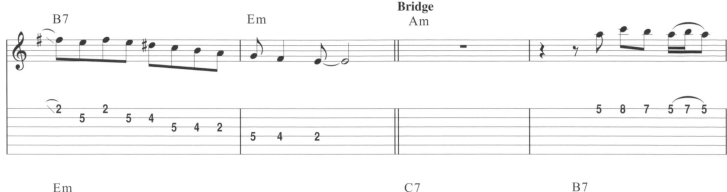

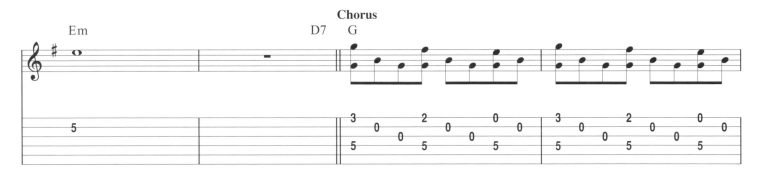

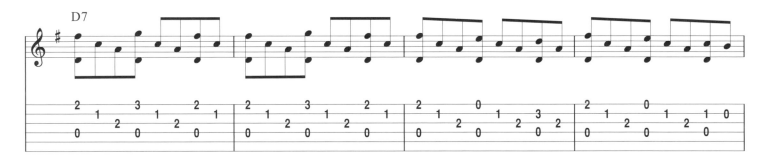

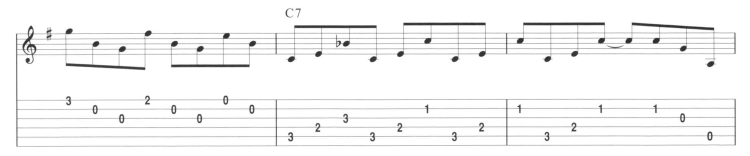

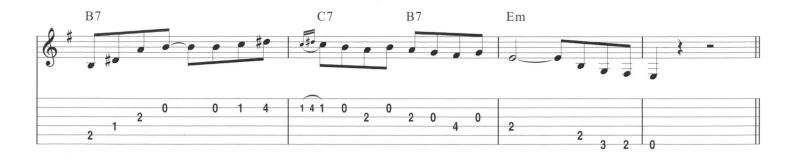

Verse

Bridge

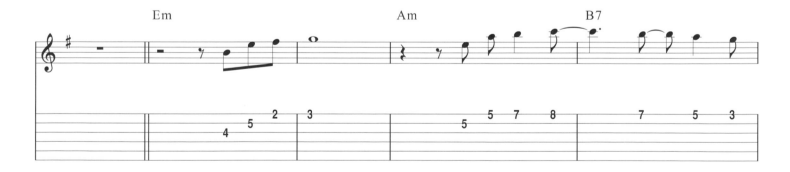

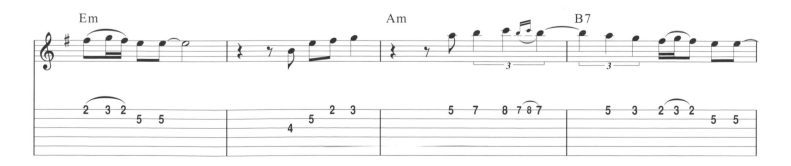

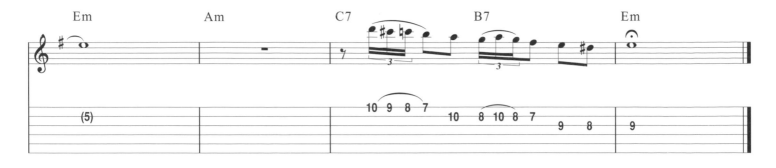

Track 57 demonstrates some sample phrases that you might like to include in your improvisations for soléa and tarantas.

TRACK 57

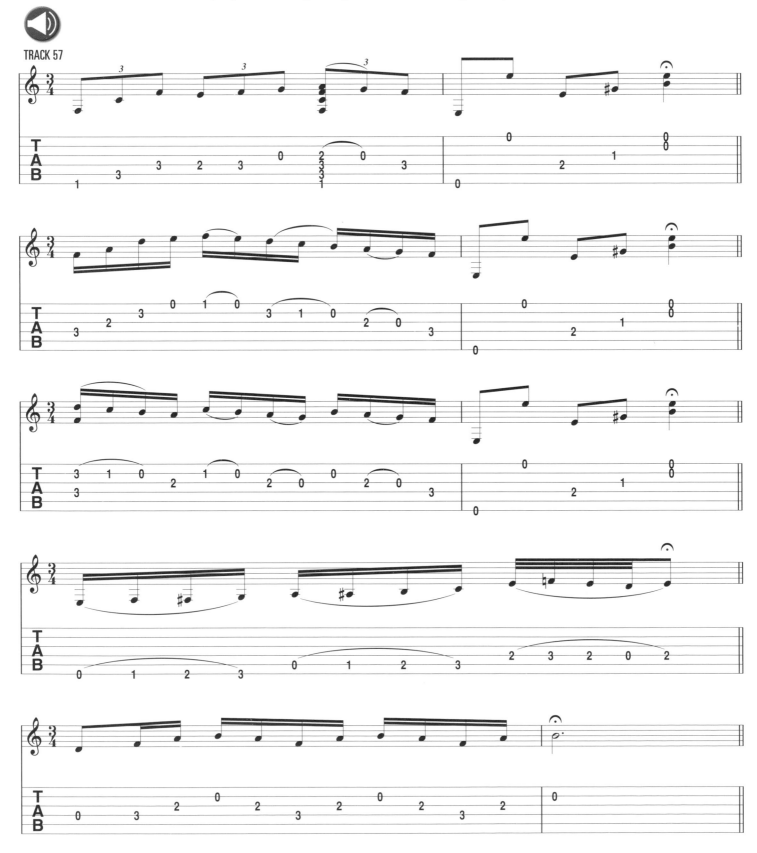

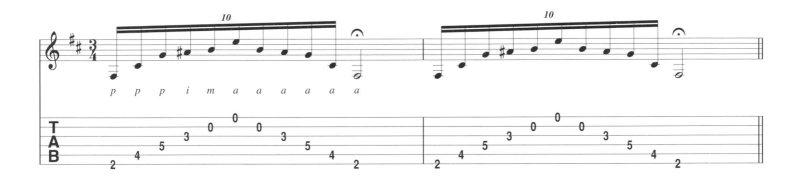

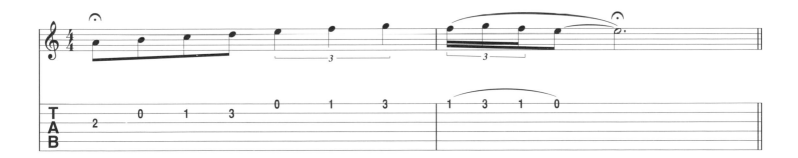

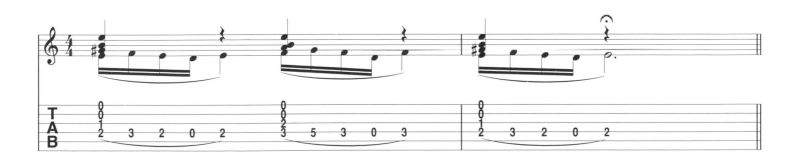

APPENDIX

THE RHYTHMS OF FLAMENCO – A SUMMARY

Rhythmically, flamenco can be divided in to three main groups, as follows:

12-beat cycle	4/4 time	3/4 time
Soleares	Farruca	Malagueñas
Alegrias	Tientos	Tarantas
Buleriás	Milonga	Sevillanas
Romeras	Taranto	Rondeña
		Fandanguillos

Originally these were the names of the dance and song forms. There are many more forms that could be included, and there are subtle differences in some of the forms. However, this rough classification will serve as a good starting point. From it, you can see that by mastering the rhythm of the soleares you can begin to understand the compás of a number of other forms, since the basic rhythmic structure remains the same.

THE CEJILLA, CAPODASTRA, OR CAPO

The capo is a device for changing (raising) the pitch of the open strings. It is placed over the strings behind a fret and holds all six strings down, acting as a mechanical barre in a similar way to a first (index) finger barre.

The capo allows the guitarist to accompany a singer in different keys without having to change the basic chord shapes into more difficult fingerings. For example, if a singer wants to perform a malagueña (normally played in the E shape) in a higher key, then the capo can be placed behind the second or third fret, raising the overall pitch of the guitar to the required key. It also adds an extra brightness to the guitar and can therefore be used to add a different tonal color.

There are a number of different types of capo on the market. The traditional flamenco capo features a straight wooden bar with a tuning peg seated in a hole in its center. A leather strap is attached to one end of the bar with a short length of plain nylon guitar string threaded through it. The strap is placed around the guitar's neck with the string inserted into the tuning peg and the wooden bar resting across the strings. Tightening the tuning peg tightens the strap, which pulls the wooden bar down onto the strings.

The capo is one of those accessories that is always being reinvented, however, and there are many different models available. Capos from the Jim Dunlop company are very popular, as are Shubb capos. A new British design, the G4 capo, is also gaining a lot of converts. The ideal capo should be easy to fit and move from one position to another, adapt easily to changes in neck profile, and it must provide a clean and positive barre without affecting the relative tuning.

Tip: Check the tuning with the capo fitted, as the pressure on the strings can affect the pitch.

HAND CLAPS

In flamenco there are two types of hand claps used as percussive accompaniment:

Palmas Sordas (Deaf hand claps): This is a softer style played with cupped hands. ▶

◀ Palmas Fuertes (Strong hand claps): Three extended fingers of the right hand are played against the cupped palm of the left hand, producing a loud, bright sound.

GLOSSARY

Alegrias ● joyful song and dance derived from soleares 12-beat cycle

Alzapúa ● technique using strokes of the thumb (like a plectrum) up and down

Anular (a) ● ring or third finger

Apagado ● muting the strings

Apoyando ● rest stroke—the right-hand finger plays a string and comes to rest on the string below

Arpeggio ● notes of chord placed one after the other

Aspazo ● to mute the strings

Ayudado ● picking technique with thumb and index finger

Bailador/Bailadora ● dancer

Baile ● the dance

Barre ● fretting several strings with a single finger across the fretboard

Boca ● guitar soundhole

Buleriás ● fast and high-spirited song and dance form performed in strict time

Cabeza ● guitar headstock

Cadence ● a resting point or closure within a sequence of chords

Cajón ● wooden, box-like percussion instrument

Cantador/Cantadora ● singer

Cante ● song

Cante Adelante • song without dance

Cante Atrás • song with dance

Cante Chico • light song

Cante Grande • serious "deep" song

Cante Jondo • profound and meaningful song

Castañuelas • castanets

Cejillas (Capodastra) • capo

Cejilla de Cabeza • guitar nut

Chiquito (c or e) • pinky or fourth finger

Clavijas • tapered wooden tuning pegs

Compás • rhythm, beat, or tempo—the compás is the accented rhythm pattern in a song or dance

Copla • verse

Cuerdas • guitar strings

Diapasón • guitar fingerboard

Duende • spirit in folk music or dancing

Falseta • melodic variations on the guitar

Fandango • light song and dance form

Fandanguillos • song and dance form in 3/4 meter

Farruca • dramatic song and dance form in 4/4 meter

Flamenco • music and dance style from Andalusia and southern Spain

Flamenco Negra • rosewood flamenco guitar

Gaujiras • song and dance form influenced by Cuban rhythms

Gitano • Spanish gypsy

Golpe • accented tap on the guitar

Golpeador • sheet of thin, clear plastic, glued to the top of the guitar between the bridge and the end of the fingerboard—the golpeador protects the table while performing the rasgueado and golpe

Indicio (i) • index or first finger

Jaleos • shouts

Juerga • a gathering of people to enjoy the music

Ligado • slur technique where notes are played by the left hand alone

Llamada • rhythmic movement in a dance signaling a change in section

Malagueñas • free-form song and dance style in 3/4 meter

Mastil • guitar neck

Medio (m) • middle or second finger

Milonga • song and dance form in 4/4 rhythm

Mode • modes are derived from scales, and each mode defines a set of intervallic relationships that create certain moods

Palillo • stick for keeping rhythm

Palmas • hand clapping

Phrygian mode • the third mode of the major scale, often used in flamenco forms—an altered version with the third note raised by one semitone is also used

Picado • picking using the i and m fingers alternately

Pito • finger snapping

Puente • guitar bridge

Pulgar (p) • thumb

Punteado • each note plucked separately

Rasgueado • rhythmic strumming

Remate • final song

Rest Stroke (apoyando) • the right-hand finger plays a string and comes to rest on the string below

Romeras • song and dance form with 12-beat cycle

Rondeñas • free-form song and dance style in 3/4 meter that involves alternate tunings

Rumbas • song form with roots in New World rhythms

Salida • short melodic phrase

Seguiriyas • dark and serious song and dance form performed in strict time

Sevillanas • song and dance form in 3/4 meter

Soleares/Soleá • song and dance form consisting of 12 beats with specific accents

Tacón • guitar neck heel

Taconeo • heel tapping

Tango • song and dance form in 4/4 rhythm; has many variations

Tanguillos • dark and serious song and dance form; derived from the tango

Tarantas • free-form song and dance style in 3/4 meter; known for its distinctive use of the minor 2nd interval

Taranto • song and dance form in 4/4 meter

Tientos • song and dance form derived from the tango

Tocador (Guitarrista) • guitarist

Toque • flamenco played on the guitar

Toque con Compás • a piece with a fixed ryhthm

Toque Libre • a piece without a fixed ryhthm

Trastes • guitar frets

Tremolo • technique of sustaining tones with rapid picking

Zapateado • heel and foot stamping

CONCLUSION

As musicians we are always searching for inspiration, new ideas, and different approaches to what we do. For me, the power of flamenco rhythms, the rich harmonies, and the deeply emotional melodies always have an uplifting effect. The study of flamenco can last a lifetime. I hope this introduction to the subject encourages you to go deeper into the music.

If you have any questions about this book please email me at hugh@acousticmasters.com or visit our website (www.acoustic-masters.com) for other guitar-related material.

—Hugh Burns
London, UK, 2008

ABOUT THE AUTHOR

Hugh Burns has been a successful studio musician for over twenty-five years. He has released six solo CDs, played with many leading artists, and recorded and toured in over thirty countries. His work can be heard on more than a hundred major film and TV soundtracks. Over forty of his own compositions have been recorded.

He has studied Spanish classical guitar for many years, has a deep interest in flamenco, and has been fortunate enough to meet and learn from a number of flamenco masters.

His latest venture is a video and record company called Acoustic Masters, dedicated to promoting and recording live performances of acoustic music.

CREDITS

Accompanying audio recorded, mixed, and mastered at Acoustic Masters Studio 1.

Engineering and mastering by Terry Relph-Knight.

Percussion tracks recorded at SAE studios, engineering by Stewart Elliot.

Text preparation: Terry Relph-Knight

Spanish language consultant: Gaspar González

Recording equipment used:

Rode NT1a and NT5 microphones, ST Audio DSP 2000 C Port ADC/DAC, Logic multitrack software, Magix Samplitude Professional 7.11 multitrack software, Roxio Easy CD Creator 5 Platinum, Zoom RhythmTrak 234 drum machine, 2GHz P4 computer with 1GB memory and 140GB disc running MS Windows XP SP2, Behringer MX802A mixer, Sennheiser HD600 headphones, Altec Lansing ACS45.1 monitors.

Instruments used:

Conde flamenco Cypress and Conde flamenco Negra guitars
D'Addario medium tension strings
Drums – Cajón, Bongos, and Congas

Special thanks to:

Daisaku Ikeda for wonderful encouragement over many years, Connie Filippello for all the support, Stewart Elliot for percussion, James Sleigh at Artemis, and Pedro Maldonado—guitar maker.